DISASTERS
THAT CHANGED
AUSTRALIA

RICHARD EVANS

VICTORY BOOKS
An imprint of Melbourne University Publishing Limited
187 Grattan Street, Carlton, Victoria 3053, Australia
mup-info@unimelb.edu.au
www.mup.com.au

First published 2009
Text © Richard Evans 2009
Design and typography © Melbourne University Publishing Limited 2009

This book is copyright. Apart from any use permitted under the *Copyright Act 1968* and subsequent amendments, no part may be reproduced, stored in a retrieval system or transmitted by any means or process whatsoever without the prior written permission of the publisher.

Every attempt has been made to locate the copyright holders for material quoted in this book. Any person or organisation that may have been overlooked or misattributed may contact the publisher.

Designed by Designland, Andrew Budge
Typeset by TypeSkill
Printed in Australia by Griffin Press, SA

National Library of Australia Cataloguing-in-Publication entry:

Disasters that changed Australia / Richard Evans.

9780522856491 (pbk)

Bibliography.

Disasters—Australia
Natural disasters—Australia.
Forest fires—Australia.
Australia—History.

363.340994

CONTENTS

	INTRODUCTION	v
1.	DIVINE WIND: CYCLONE TRACY, 1974	1
2.	'JUST SLAUGHTER': FLANDERS, 1917	21
3.	DESTROYING THE PROMISED LAND: THE GREAT RESOURCE CRASH, c. 40 000 BC	57
4.	THE TASMANIAN GENOCIDE: 1804–1838	69
5.	FERAL NATION: RABBITS, 1859 TO THE PRESENT	85
6.	BLACK FRIDAY, 1939 AND BEYOND	103
7.	THE DEPRESSION: 1930–1939	123
8.	THE GREAT WHITE ELEPHANT: THE SNOWY MOUNTAINS SCHEME, 1949–1974	141
9.	FOOL'S GOLD: MONTREAL OLYMPIC GAMES, 1976	155
10.	THE GREAT DROUGHT: 2002 TO THE PRESENT	167
	SOURCES AND FURTHER READING	179
	ACKNOWLEDGEMENTS	197

INTRODUCTION

As I write, smoke from the worst bushfires in Australia's history hangs over my city. It filters the light of the sun, giving everything a golden tinge. It would be quite pretty, if you did not know what had caused it, if you did not know that the police are still recovering the charred remains of people who, two days ago, died horribly.

Some of the fires are still burning and the dead are still not counted, but already there is bitter argument. Without exception, it seems, the disaster of Black Saturday has confirmed our prejudices. Climate change sceptics blame 'greeny councils' who would not allow fuel-reduction burning. Fundamentalist Christians say that this is biblical—the wrath of God, punishment for Victoria's recent decision to decriminalise abortion. For environmentalists, this is global warming in action: the shape of things to come. People are hurting, angry, searching for someone to blame.

Disasters do this. They divide and traumatise society. In the anger and grief of the aftermath, people reveal themselves and what divides them. The picture is not always flattering.

There is another side, of course, as the response to the bushfires has shown: the heroism and dedication of those who fight the fires and help the wounded and dispossessed; the spontaneous generosity of the wider public; the determination of small communities to rebuild. Astonishing stories of survival capture our imagination. Fundraising events become celebrations of community spirit.

It is not yet clear how Black Saturday will change Australia—but it will. That is something else disasters do: they are agents of change.

The ancient Greeks had two words to describe time. There is *chronos*, ordinary time: the ticking of a clock, the passage of the sun in the sky. And then there is *kairos*, usually translated as 'critical time' but it is something more than that. Kairos time is a rupture in the state of the world, the moment when everything changes.

For an individual, kairos might be a serious car accident: people dead, brain injury, charges, jail. There is a break: life before, then life after what those affected will come to call 'the Accident'. Kairos may last a few seconds, but it also endures, sometimes without end. The Accident will be with those it touches for years, perhaps whole lives. It will revisit, in nightmares and daydreams. Some fail to adjust—'She never recovered'—while others succeed in making a new life. But still, the Accident defines them, becomes part of their being.

A major disaster is kairos on a grand scale. It is a rupture in how we understand the world and ourselves, not just for individuals or a small group, but for society as a whole. The people of Darwin talk about things happening 'before Tracy' or 'after

Tracy': the cyclone is a fault line in the city's past. For the survivors of World War I, the world before August 1914 was like a lost paradise, a golden time before the human race went mad.

But in historical terms, disasters are not aberrations. There is no 'normal' state of affairs which a disaster disturbs before things 'return to normal'. For every society, disasters are an integral part of growth and change.

Disasters take many forms: some are the work of forces of nature, like a bushfire. Others are entirely man-made: war, economic collapse, setting rabbits loose. Some happen abruptly, others unfold over decades. Regardless, there are consistent patterns to the experience of disaster. There will, usually, be warnings of danger—which are usually ignored. There is the moment of impact, and the community's immediate response. And last comes the hardest part: accepting that we live in the aftermath of a terrible event, and learning from it, especially learning what we did wrong—a social and political struggle over what the disaster *means*.

Disasters have an economics, a political science, a theology and a psychology. Above all, they have a history—or rather, two histories. There is the messy reality of what happened, and there is a comforting story which allows us to handle that reality.

Attempting to understand and assimilate the tragedy of World War I, Australia created the legend of the digger and a sacred day. We remember the Depression as a time of suffering, but also as a time when Australians pulled together and looked out for their neighbours. Any account of Cyclone Tracy will laud the generosity of the rest of Australia in helping the distressed people of Darwin.

As inevitable as the regrowth after a bushfire, an Australian disaster will produce stories which affirm the essential goodness of the Australian people. We will discover, again, that we are stoic, brave and resourceful, good in a crisis. In the short term, this is perhaps socially necessary: it helps us recover our morale and start rebuilding. But too often in Australia, we never go beyond this point. If there is blame, we lay it with foolish individuals, or with negligent officials who fail in their duty to protect the community. There is rarely any searching examination of the wider community, of our attitudes and beliefs and patterns of behaviour.

Australian disasters have often been much worse than they needed to be, because we ignored credible warnings. For years before the 1939 Black Friday bushfires, forestry officers urged timber millers to build dugouts to protect their workers. But by the time the fire came, many had not bothered, and dozens of mill workers died.

There are many examples of disasters that could have been averted. As long ago as the 1960s, experts warned that urban Australia was wasting water, that we had no business hosing down cars and driveways and growing rose bushes in the driest of continents. It took a catastrophic drought at the beginning of this century before we paid much notice.

Even worse, our response to disaster has sometimes been angry denial that there was a disaster at all. We celebrate the audacious engineering of the Snowy Mountains Hydro-Electric Scheme, but explain away its high economic and environmental costs with vague talk of national pride. We celebrate the courage of the Anzacs charging up the cliffs of Gallipoli, but pay much less attention to the pointless slaughter of the Western Front, suicidal campaigns which were fully supported by an Australian prime minister who fiercely denounced any attempt to negotiate peace.

+++

This book is the result of a long personal journey as a writer and an historian. Exploring Australia's past—a lifelong fascination—has brought with it the realisation that many of the comforting myths I grew up with do not withstand scrutiny. These myths are resilient: they are the basis for the official *Guide to Becoming an Australian Citizen*, which takes the prospective Aussie on a feel-good tour through a national past of explorers and gold, Simpson and his donkey, Phar Lap and Federation, the Snowy Mountains and multiculturalism. The story is far more complex and sharp-edged than that, and far more interesting.

Australia needs to re-examine its past, peel back the familiar comforting stories, and rethink how it has responded to disaster. We need to learn from our mistakes, especially from our signature mistake: the belief that we have nothing to learn.

Richard Evans
Melbourne, 9 February 2009

Cyclone Tracy was a hair-raising experience. The destruction of Darwin by Cyclone Tracy was almost total.
(National Library of Australia and The Herald and Weekly Times Photographic Collection)

1
DIVINE WIND: CYCLONE TRACY, 1974

Darkness. Complete darkness, and the roar of the wind. These were the overwhelming memories of the survivors of Cyclone Tracy. Darkness, rarely experienced in the modern world, of a mineshaft, or a grave. And the roar: some people compared it to a thousand freight trains, or a jet engine in the lounge room.

In the small hours of Christmas morning, 1974, most of the 43 000 people who lived in Darwin found themselves in shrieking blackness, their roofs and walls being peeled away by the storm, soaked to the skin by torrential rain, wondering if they were going to live. Decades later, one survivor recalled: 'We learned to pray'.

+ + +

Half a century ago, the writer Ernestine Hill called Darwin 'the crazy little capital of the land of lost endeavour'. That land was the Northern Territory, the 'problem child of empire, land of an ever-shadowed past and an ever-shining future, of an eternal promise that never comes true'.

The Northern Territory was an afterthought. During the nineteenth century, as the colonies of Queensland, South Australia and Western Australia were formed, arbitrary lines were drawn on the map, cutting across vast reaches of arid land—much of it still unknown to Europeans—with the careless authority of the imperial age. The Northern Territory was the bit that was left, up the top and in the middle, which no-one much wanted. Its boundary with Western Australia was finally decided in 1921.

There are people who love Darwin—Ernestine Hill was one of them—but there are a great many others who hate it. Roland Herman Milford, a gloomy ex-soldier who worked there in the late 1920s, was scathing in his portrayal:

> A sweating, soaking day in December. Many of the living corpses of Darwin in a comatose state of alcoholism. Blacks, half-castes, pearlshell-divers, government officials ... and others—all stagger or lurch unevenly about in the poisoned air as [if] each movement of their bloated, beer-soaked bodies was going to be their [last] ... a vague atmosphere of immorality pervading everything.

Milford was a bit of a whinger. In 1932 he drove a car right around Australia and wrote a travel book about the trip in which he complains about almost every place he visits. The malaise he describes in Darwin, however, was real enough.

Darwin is one of those places which exists because of where it is—for strategic reasons. It has played a vital role in Australia's communications and defence. As a result it has, for the whole of its history, been a place where people are posted: by government agencies, or large companies, or the defence forces. This is not true of the Aboriginal population, of course, but for most other inhabitants, Darwin remains quasi-colonial, a sort of transit lounge for nation builders from the populated southern cities. People come, work for a few years, and then leave.

Ernestine Hill again: 'In its glorious setting, Darwin was unloved and unlovely. Apart from a few faithfuls, there were only two classes—those paid to stay and those without ... money to go'.

Part of the problem is the weather. For half the year it is hot and dry, while for the other half it is hot and wet. The weather forecast for Darwin has become something of a national joke: during winter it is '32 degrees and sunny', during summer it's '32 degrees, humid, late storms'. To many Australians accustomed to the more moderate southern climes, the wet season especially is enervating and oppressive. In the days before air conditioning, in a society which insisted on dress that covered all but the head and hands, the level of discomfort was extreme.

And then there was the potential for weather like nothing a temperate climate could produce: the tropical cyclone.

The tipping point is 27 degrees Celsius. When seawater reaches this temperature, tropical cyclones can form.

The tipping point is 27 degrees Celsius. When seawater reaches this temperature, tropical cyclones can form. What is needed is a warm sea and relatively still air, thick with moisture. The heat makes the air rise and as it does so, the water vapour condenses into droplets, forming clouds. When water changes from a gas to a liquid, energy is released that further heats the air, which continues to rise. The column of rising air draws in more moist air and the cycle continues, building up huge thunderheads crackling with electricity.

Usually the result is a heavy dumping of afternoon rain, a clockwork occurrence in the tropical wet season. But if, at high altitude, a strong cross-wind whips away the top of the rising column of hot air, then the inflow of air continues and the formless masses of heavy rain clouds are pulled into a tightening vortex. Like a rotating ice-skater, speeding up as she pulls in her arms, the wind gathers speed. Around a centre of very low air pressure, the 'eye', ever stronger winds spiral in, pulling moist air from over the surrounding sea, releasing water vapour, giving off staggering amounts of energy and powering an extreme weather system. This is what is called a typhoon in Asia, a hurricane in North America, and, in Australia, a tropical cyclone.

Like a rotating ice-skater, speeding up as she pulls in her arms, the wind gathers speed.

Once it has formed, a cyclone will begin to move, like a coin spinning on a table. The usual course for a cyclone in the southern hemisphere is a slow southerly curve, heading west at first, then looping back to the east. However, the course can be erratic and is very difficult to predict.

About thirty cyclones will form in a typical year, with about three of those in Australian waters. Many peter out after a few hours or days, and bring little more than heavy rain. But some retain their intensity. If they hit a coastal city, the damage and loss of life can be immense. In 1876, a cyclone off the coast of modern Bangladesh caused flooding which drowned 100 000 people; as many died from disease in the storm's aftermath. The low-lying Texas city of Galveston was hit by a hurricane in 1900 that killed 6000 people. Japan is periodically affected by cyclones. In 1934 a cyclone struck Osaka, destroying more than 45 000 houses and killing 3000 people.

Cyclones have a special place in Japanese history. In 1281 AD, a huge Mongol fleet attacked the islands, landing an army in Kyushu. A cyclone struck the fleet and almost completely destroyed it. In gratitude for what they saw as a miracle, the Japanese called the storm 'the Divine Wind', or 'kamikaze'.

CITY OF NINE LIVES

> The crash of buildings and the rattle of iron and timber falling about, combined with the blinding rain and the roaring of the tempest, was an experience those who underwent it will never forget to their dying day. Strongly built houses collapsed like houses of cards; roofs blew bodily away; lamp and telegraph posts were bent or torn up; immense beams of timber were hurled away like chaff; trees were uprooted; in many instances large houses were lifted bodily from their foundations and deposited ten and twelve feet away; and in short, the night was one of terrifying destructiveness that made the stoutest heart quail.

This is a description of a cyclone that destroyed Darwin, written by a journalist at the *NT Times*. The winds were so terrific that only a few buildings escaped destruction and even they lost their roofs or were otherwise seriously damaged. The fury of the storm almost defied comprehension: a flagstaff, which was set in three feet of concrete, 'was blown out of the ground, concrete and all'. This was not Tracy but a cyclone which hit Darwin on the night of 6 January 1896. The number of people killed is uncertain, but may have been as many as sixty.

The South Australian Government, which then administered the Northern Territory, was both slow and niggardly. The shortage of liveable accommodation in Darwin led to overcrowding—most people had been left homeless—and as the wet season continued, disease began to spread among the inhabitants. A full year after the cyclone, public servants were still trying to work in offices which leaked every time it rained. Not for the last time, the people of Darwin felt abandoned by masters in a distant capital.

In March 1937, the town was again hit by a cyclone. This storm was less severe—there was only one recorded death—but significant damage was still caused. Again the town was rebuilt—Ernestine Hill called it 'the place of nine lives'—only to be again destroyed, this time by Japanese bombs during World War II.

The first Japanese bombing raids on Darwin, on 19 February 1942, have an unusual place in Australian memory, not least because they were the subject of a massive cover-up.

The attacks, which involved more than 180 aircraft, came as a complete surprise. The raiders had been seen passing Bathurst Island and the RAAF station at Darwin was alerted by radio telephone. However, the commander there thought the planes were probably American, and did not pass the warning on or sound the alert. In two waves, one beginning at 10 a.m.

and the second just before noon, Japanese bombs and machine guns caused terrible damage to the town, the airfield, and shipping in the harbour. Eight ships were sunk, including a US Navy destroyer, and three others were badly damaged. Much of the harbour wharf was destroyed. Most of the public buildings in town were wrecked. The RAAF base suffered badly: nine military aircraft were smashed on the ground; the airfield's hangars and repair shops were ruined; a dump holding 300 000 rounds of ammunition exploded. In all, 243 people were thought to have been killed, but the true total may have been greater; more than 300 people were wounded.

In two waves, one beginning at 10 a.m. and the second just before noon, Japanese bombs and machine guns caused terrible damage to the town, the airfield, and shipping in the harbour.

The legend of Aussie courage under fire took a battering that day in Darwin. Some people behaved bravely. The crews of anti-aircraft guns, most of whom had never seen action before, stayed at their stations and put up the only effective resistance to the raids. The nurses at the hospital, which was itself attacked, showed great devotion to their duty. Other individuals, including a prisoner in Fanny Bay Gaol who was released to help with the rescue effort, were later singled out by a royal commission for their courage and sacrifice.

As a whole, though, the response to the raid was a debacle. In the wake of the bombing, rumours swept the town that a Japanese invasion was imminent. Civil order broke down: there was looting and panic. About half the civilian population sought to flee south by any vehicle available—even the municipal sanitary carts were used—or on foot. The royal commissioner who investigated the raids, Charles Lowe, reported: 'I myself observed in the Darwin Hotel tables upon which drinks remained half-consumed, letters started but not finished ... and other signs of a very hasty exit'.

Most embarrassing was the number of military servicemen who joined the rout. Many RAAF personnel, in particular, abandoned their posts and the airfield was soon practically deserted. Many fled into the bush, others headed for towns further south. One man, in what Lowe dryly called 'an extreme feat', turned up thirteen days later in Melbourne. The whole affair, he wrote, was 'deplorable'.

The response of the Australian authorities was to cover it up. Newspaper accounts gave the death toll as seventeen, vastly overstated the Japanese losses, and concealed the panic altogether. The affair remained a sensitive topic for decades: Lowe's report remained closed to public access until the 1960s.

In the wake of World War II, Australia consciously set about the task of nation building. It was the era of the Snowy Mountains Hydro-Electric Scheme and mass migration, the fostering of heavy industry and universities, and the vast expansion of Australia's cities. Darwin was one obvious place to set to work. Old timers like Ernestine Hill hated the whole thing: 'Let them sing anthems to that mythical new Darwin, model tropical bungalows, air-conditioned suburbs, poinciana parks and palatial hotels, a garden city cut and dried, Front Gate of Australia that never yet came true'.

What eventuated was both less impersonal and less well-built than Hill's imagined model city. Darwin remained sleepy. Many of the new suburbs, built to house the public servants who mostly stayed only for a few years, had a fair amount of the shabby, jerry-built 'old Darwin' about them. Most houses were raised on posts to take advantage of the breeze. The windows were glass louvres that allowed air to flow through, the roofs were corrugated iron, the walls made of sheets of fibrocement. Below the house might be a laundry block of hollow concrete bricks. Though plain, the buildings were set in the lush gardens that tropical climate encouraged, and were pleasant enough to live in.

Many were poorly built. Even those builders who were skilled and conscientious were creating buildings completely unsuitable for a city which had twice been hit by tropical cyclones and which, in 1974, was about due for another.

'VERY DESTRUCTIVE WINDS'

On 1 December 1974, about 350 kilometres north-west of Darwin in the Timor Sea, a low pressure system developed into Tropical Cyclone Selma. Selma moved directly towards Darwin and two days later was only 100 kilometres away. The Bureau of Meteorology issued a steady stream of alerts, warning the people of Darwin to prepare for a potentially devastating storm. But at 10 a.m. on 3 December, Selma changed direction, swinging north and then west away from the city. There had been a lot of rain and some trees had been brought down, but nothing too alarming.

It is a common pattern in disasters: the near miss which causes complacency. When authorities warn of a serious danger which does not eventuate, people can become fatally sceptical. One Darwin resident recalled an early conversation about whether Tracy was a real threat: 'We had had Cyclone Selma only a few weeks before ... Everyone was sick of talking about cyclones—and besides, Christmas was here'.

Everyone was sick of talking about cyclones—and besides, Christmas was here'.

On 21 December, a large cloud mass that had been forming in the Arafura Sea, some 700 kilometres to the north-east of Darwin, began to revolve and the winds at its centre reached high velocities. At 10 p.m. the system started to move and it was officially designated a tropical cyclone, and given the name Tracy.

Another resident recalled that like most people, he was concerned that bad weather would spoil Christmas. At Christmas Eve parties, the consensus was that Tracy would do what Selma had done on approaching Darwin, what every cyclone for decades had done: veer away. The police were in touch with the Weather Bureau and had followed standard procedures to prepare for an emergency. But no-one was really worried. 'It was still being taken lightly', one officer recalled. 'It was "just another blow".'

By noon on 24 December, the picture was clearer, and alarming. Tracy was 110 kilometres north-west of Darwin and was headed south-east—straight for the city. The winds inside the storm were extreme. At 12.30 p.m. the Tropical Cyclone Warning Centre issued a formal alert:

VERY DESTRUCTIVE WINDS OF 120 KILOMETRES
PER HOUR WITH GUSTS TO 150 KILOMETRES PER HOUR
HAVE BEEN REPORTED NEAR THE CENTRE
AND ARE EXPECTED IN THE DARWIN AREA TONIGHT
AND TOMORROW.

Some people took precautions: putting masking tape on windows, tying down loose objects, checking that they had a battery torch and radio in case the power went out. Others attended Christmas parties, got drunk, and went to bed.

What then unfolded was a slow-building nightmare. As evening drew into night, power was lost, the wind rose, and kept rising, and the torrential rain forced its way into houses. At first, people tried to protect carpets and valuables, but such thoughts were soon forgotten as the magnitude of the storm became apparent. Glass louvres bowed with the pressure of the wind, and began to explode. Many windows were ripped—frame and all—from the walls. Most families retreated to the bathroom—by conventional wisdom and official advice, the strongest and safest room in the house.

After midnight, the full fury of the leading edge of the cyclone struck. The wind reached speeds in excess of 150 kilometres per hour. Many houses lost their roofs, either as cladding was peeled up then whipped away, or with the whole roof suddenly being lifted and swept into the darkness. With the torrential rain now soaking internal partitions, and the structure of houses weakened, walls collapsed or were blown away. Debris—and this included objects as big as refrigerators—hurtled through the air, shattering houses downwind, causing more debris and a chain of destruction.

At about 3 a.m., the eye of the cyclone passed over Darwin, bringing an eerie stillness. There was a strange light, a diffuse lightening, like St Elmo's fire. In the quiet, people could hear injured neighbours screaming.

Some houses, more protected than others, had survived the first wind. But everyone knew that this was only a brief lull. When the eye of a cyclone has passed over, the 'second wind' comes. It is often more destructive than the first wind because it comes from the opposite direction, is often stronger, and arrives abruptly. This was the case with Tracy: the first wind had built up over a period of more than an hour, but the second wind arrived like an express train, all the more shocking after the relative silence of the eye. Gusts of well over 200 kilometres per hour filled the air with debris, and blasted already damaged houses apart—in some cases the walls, the collapsed ceilings, every piece of furniture were swept away. Families were left clinging to whatever wreckage remained. Adding to their misery was the intense cold, as everything was saturated by driving rain and chilled by the gale. The bare floor of a house bucking in the storm on its poles came to be known as a 'dance floor' among survivors.

Some people tried to crawl downstairs, but there was really nowhere to go. Few houses had a cyclone shelter, and laundry blocks and sheds were often made of light concrete bricks: the walls were not reinforced and bowed in the wind. Many people ended up sheltering in their cars. This was dangerous, but where else were they to go?

Around seventy people died. Hundreds were seriously injured. Of the thousands who survived, almost everyone was wet and cold and often in pain from cuts, lacerations and broken bones. At about 6.30 a.m., after the storm had faded to a drizzling rain, a grey dawn broke over Darwin. The light revealed a scene of utter devastation.

Gary MacKay, an Army officer who was part of the relief effort and later wrote a history of the disaster, described the damage as 'almost obscene in its totality'. Some observers compared the sight to Hiroshima in the wake of the atomic bomb. One was more prosaic: 'Darwin was a 250-square-mile-rubbish dump'.

Engineers are generally careful writers and not prone to exaggeration. George Walker was commissioned to report on Cyclone Tracy's impact on buildings. 'The destruction caused in Darwin by Cyclone Tracy', he wrote, 'was the worst suffered by an Australian city in any disaster'.

By Christmas morning, Darwin had, in material terms, almost ceased to exist. For many hours the city was completely isolated from the outside world: every telephone line was cut, every radio transmitter out of action. Tracy destroyed almost every house and block of flats. It seriously damaged almost every public building: schools, hospitals, churches, office blocks and large hotels. By one estimate, of the city's 13 000 dwellings, only 400 had survived intact.

The city's vital infrastructure was destroyed or immobilised. Every roadway was blocked, the airport runway was unusable, the port's wharves wrecked. The power distribution network, most of it comprising overhead powerlines, had been demolished—the power station was badly damaged, its generators immobilised. The water supply and sewerage system both relied on electric pumps, so these also ceased to function. With no sanitation, and so few habitable buildings, there was a danger of diseases such as typhoid.

The hospital quickly ran out of basic supplies like local anaesthetic, which was badly needed as so many people had cuts that required stitches. There was water damage throughout the hospital, and in the treatment wards the floors ran red with blood.

There was water damage throughout the hospital, and in the treatment wards the floors ran red with blood.

Making matters worse for the people of Darwin, although the rest of the country responded with great generosity to the disaster, much of the assistance given was ill-considered, poorly organised and of little use. The civil authorities were astonished and dismayed when planes arrived in the sweltering tropical city loaded with blankets. Alan Reiher, a public servant with the Board of Works who played a major role in the relief effort, later said that 'most of the things which came in during the first few days (except food and medical supplies) were not wanted'.

It quickly became obvious that the city would have to be almost entirely evacuated. All 'non-essential people' were airlifted out. The mass evacuation of some 20 000 people, and their temporary accommodation in military barracks, migrant hostels and private homes across the country, was a vast undertaking.

The devastation of Darwin was so great that the federal government seriously considered abandoning the city altogether and rebuilding somewhere else. Katherine was one possibility. As it was, a reconstruction commission was created and a new city arose. Despite the bitter wrangling over what form the fifth 'new Darwin' should take, the reconstruction is now generally remembered as a success.

'Darwin is one of the great cities of Australia', said Rex Patterson, then Minister for the Northern Territory, on the thirtieth anniversary of Tracy. 'It proved that the decision to rebuild Darwin was a good one.' Marshall Perron, a Northern Territory politician who later served as Chief Minister, said that the disaster also provided opportunity: 'Lots of dead wood was blown away, and this allowed a fresh start'.

Tracy is sometimes seen as having been the catalyst for the NT achieving self-government, and for a more permanent and settled community. Another Chief Minister, Clare Martin, exemplified this cheery view. In 2004 she wrote: 'In many ways Tracy transformed Darwin from an isolated tropical outpost, operated by a legion of Commonwealth public servants, to a modern tropical city determined to become Australia's Gateway to Asia'.

There are shades of the hollow boosterism satirised by Ernestine Hill in all of this. Certainly it puts a gloss on the human suffering created by the disaster, and its long-term economic and social cost. It also avoids the sober truth: old Darwin should have survived Tracy more or less intact.

It would have done so if the sensible warnings of intelligent and responsible people had been heeded.

NO-ONE BELIEVED IT COULD HAPPEN TO THEM

Tracy was a cyclone of immense destructive power, but in no way can it be seen as a freak event. That a severe cyclone would again hit Darwin was certain; the only question was when. Yet the city, in its physical and social structures, was appallingly ill-prepared.

According to George Walker's report, large buildings, which were required to be certified for structural strength by engineers, survived the storm 'reasonably well'. Smaller buildings, which included almost every house in Darwin, 'performed extremely badly'. Perhaps 60 per cent of houses were damaged beyond repair 'and in some of the northern suburbs the destruction was nearly 100 per cent'.

It was found that in some cases, window frames had not been actually fixed to the surrounding walls—they were just 'sitting there', providing no structural strength at all. But even when basic workmanship was adequate, the house designs were not. At that time, the standards required for houses built in tropical areas did provide for higher wind velocities, but were otherwise much the same as those for non-tropical areas.

Walker argued that, had buildings been properly engineered, a cyclone of Tracy's magnitude still would have caused significant damage, but would have destroyed less than 5 per cent of the houses—still a disaster, but on a far smaller scale. Fewer people would have died or been left homeless. More of the city's basic infrastructure would have remained intact. The added trauma of mass evacuation might have been avoided.

The things which should have been done, but were not, were basic.

Three years before Tracy, in December 1971, Cyclone Althea had hit Townsville, causing significant damage. The Department of Works in Darwin had drawn on this experience. They recommended that extra strengthening be provided to houses, that cladding be better secured, and that windows be protected with shutters and screens. But no-one paid much attention.

The main reason was complacency. As Alan Reiher recalled, 'No-one in Darwin believed it could happen to them. No-one as far as we could find had experienced a severe cyclone in Darwin before'.

The cost of the relief operation and the reconstruction of Darwin was immense. Estimates vary from $600 million to more than $1 billion. Such a massive diversion of resources was a major setback in the development of basic infrastructure in other parts of the Northern Territory. The 'modern tropical city' of Darwin sucked badly needed resources from Katherine, Alice Springs and many remote communities. Even on a national basis, the reconstruction of Darwin cut into resources for development: $1 billion paid for a lot of roads, schools and hospitals in 1975.

In one important respect, though, Tracy did change Australia for the better. In wiping Darwin off the map, the cyclone made the rest of the country far more aware of the city, and of Australia's northern tropics, than had ever been the case before.

Three days after the disaster, Prime Minister Gough Whitlam declared that the shock had awakened a new sense of community: 'it is an Australian tragedy which transcends politics, state boundaries and personal differences'. Australians everywhere, he said, 'are responding spontaneously and generously to the call for help'.

Historian Brad West argues that Tracy was a defining moment in the creation of Australian national identity, having the sort of impact that foreign invasion has had on other societies. It is an irony that it took a natural disaster to have this impact when the 1942 bombing *was* an attack by a hostile nation.

It is also ironic that Tracy is remembered primarily as an 'act of God'. Histories of the event focus on tales of survival and suffering, with the partly happy ending of a revitalised Darwin. This picture is true so far as it goes, but there is an uglier underside.

Like most 'natural' disasters, the devastation wreaked by Tracy was largely a human construction. In a city which twice previously had been battered by cyclones, it should not have required another one to convince us to change our ways.

At the end of George Walker's report, after many pages discussing purlins and trusses, cladding strength and lateral bracing, he strays into a philosophical observation: 'It is unfortunate, but true, that one generally has to experience a disaster to be really convinced of the need to avoid one'.

It is a tragedy of Australian history that Walker is right.

Men, horses and wreckage on the Flanders battlefield, 1917.
The Flanders offensive was by far Australia's bloodiest military operation.
(Australian War Memorial Negative Number H09281)

2 'JUST SLAUGHTER': FLANDERS, 1917

In Preston, the northern suburb of Melbourne where I live, there is a large war memorial. It is a red-brick pavilion, like a heavy-duty gazebo. It's imposing, even impressive, but in truth, rather ugly. It stands in front of the town hall, in the middle of a busy shopping strip, but hardly anyone, regardless of race or creed, pays the war memorial much attention.

The near-invisibility of the memorial is appropriate. It cannot achieve its purpose because that purpose was to make understandable loss beyond comprehension, and to give meaning and reason to a disaster which had neither.

In Europe, where those who are war heroes to one community might be considered genocidal criminals in the next village, war memorials can cause serious tension. Some nationalist groups will blow up memorials to which they take offence. There is even a word for it in German—*denkmalsturz*, 'monument fall'. Australians have a less dramatic approach to *denkmalsturz*. Lacking the nerve to publicly challenge the meaning of a memorial, we maintain it just well enough to avoid being accused of neglect, and forget what it really means.

Inside the Preston memorial are eight large marble plaques. On them are carved rows and rows and rows of names. On the right are the men who served overseas during the Great War, and who returned. On the left: those who did not return.

The numbers are staggering. Preston was semirural in 1914, a fringe suburb where the main employers were dairy farms and tanneries. This small community sent 372 men to serve overseas. Ninety of them—almost one in four—were killed.

Behind each name, neatly carved and painted black, what pain must lie.

Mehegan, J, served abroad and returned. Mehegan, F, was killed. Mehegan, TWJ, was killed. Crumond, A, and Crumond, B, were both killed. Crumond, JB, returned. And on, and on.

Were they brothers? Cousins? Fathers and sons? Did they die in the same battle, or many months apart—and which would have been worse for the people who loved them? What was it like for JB Crumond and J Mehegan and the others who returned: did they feel grateful, guilty, scarred?

I once met a geriatric nurse who told me of a patient, a woman in her nineties. Deaf, senile and almost blind, once or twice every day, she would loudly say, as if answering a question, 'He died in France!' Who was he? Husband? Brother? Lover? No-one knew except the old woman, and she never said. She would be silent for hours, and then: 'He died in France!'

Some 43 000 Australians died in France and Belgium, in 1917 especially, and something of Australia died there too.

The Australian memory of World War I is dominated by the legend of Gallipoli. Each Anzac Day, the significance of the Gallipoli campaign to Australia is re-emphasised until it reaches the ridiculous. 'On 25 April 1915 a new world was born', says an essay on the official Anzac Day website. 'A new side of man's character was revealed. The Spirit of ANZAC was kindled. It flared with a previously unknown, almost superhuman strength.'

On the strength of such hyperbole, Anzac Cove has become a standard stop for young Australians on the international backpacker trail, though often at the cost of a descent into crass, boozy self-parody. Most Australians know we were at Gallipoli fighting 'the Turks', but would be hard-pressed to say why. Popular accounts of the Western Front tend to skip over a lot of what happened, mentioning the Australians' baptism of fire at Pozieres, on the Somme, in 1916, then getting as quickly as possible to 1918, when the Australian Imperial Force (AIF) fought and won battles that had some point to them.

Bullecourt: a bloody fiasco which killed six times more Australians in twenty-four hours than the entire Vietnam War.

The geography is confusing. The Preston war memorial lists battles fought in 'France' which actually took place in Belgium. Other memorials refer to 'Flanders', which is an older name for parts of Belgium and northern France. The names of battles are obscure, impenetrable: Bullecourt, Messines, Lagnicourt, Menin Road, Polygon Wood, Broodseinde, Passchendaele.

These words mean little now—'The battle of *where*?', people have often asked when I have talked about this book. But for a sacrificed generation they told the story of 1917, like stations on a train line to Hell.

Bullecourt: a bloody fiasco which killed six times more Australians in twenty-four hours than the entire Vietnam War. Messines and the others: victories, sort of, but each costing thousands and thousands of lives. And the last stop, Passchendaele: horror, almost beyond reckoning. Slaughter, pointless slaughter.

If you look at these places now on a satellite map, two things strike you: how close together they are, and how small they are—hamlets of a few dozen houses. Why were they worth fighting over? The short answer is: they weren't. The beginning of the longer answer is that Passchendaele rests on a low ridge.

Wilfred Owen, the English poet killed in the last week of the war, wrote of a group of soldiers about to go into attack.

> *Many there stood still*
> *To face the stark, blank sky beyond the ridge*
> *Knowing their feet had come to the end of the world.*

For hundreds of thousands of young men, including tens of thousands of Australians, Passchendaele would be the ridge at the end of the world.

+++

The reasons for the battles of 1917, indeed for the whole of the Great War, are rarely discussed outside a specialist historical literature. Anzac Day, the most important commemoration of the Australian military experience, focuses on the qualities of the soldiers. Official rhetoric links every conflict in which Australians have fought—from Gallipoli to Kabul via the

Kokoda Trail, Hellfire Pass, Korea and Long Tan—into one seamless narrative of courage, service and self-sacrifice.

'The spirit of the ANZACs had touched the hearts and minds of all Australians', says an RSL website.

> They couldn't stay home and do nothing after their mates had given so much. Their country needed them and they wanted to stand up and be counted. The true spirit of the ANZACs—a willingness to sacrifice their lives for their country, their pride and their mates.

But on what is, surely, the most important issue—why were we fighting?—there is only silence.

Even during the war itself, the answer to this question was never clear. The statesmen of the day spoke of helping the Mother Country and the British Empire in her hour of need. But that need was the result of the war, not justification for it.

William Morris Hughes was prime minister of Australia for most of the Great War, and was probably the most bloody-minded hardliner among all the Allied leaders, but even he never quite pinned down the reasoning. Speaking during a visit to England in 1916, he said that Australia's soldiers, who had 'bodies magnificently developed', were

> coming out to do battle for the country that made them. They are showing today the mettle of their pasture. They are fighting for everything they hold dear by land or sea. They are fighting this battle in deadly earnest, knowing it to be a battle to the death. For it is a battle from which we

will emerge triumphant, with our great Empire welded indissolubly together, or in which we must go down with all prospects of achieving our destiny forever doomed.

From this jumble, what can be gleaned? We were fighting for Australia, but why? We were fighting to preserve the British Empire, and in 1914 the Empire was important, but why, exactly, was the Empire at war? We were fighting for everything we hold dear—meaninglessness redux: a foggy description of fog.

Perhaps the most honest part of Hughes' speech spoke of how Australia's young men, their 'bodies magnificently developed', would prove 'the mettle of their pasture'. Like cattle, they would be brought into peak condition, then sent to the slaughterhouse.

'The war changed their lives', the Anzac Day website says of the Australian soldiers. 'But it also changed the lives of the many French and Belgian civilians who lived in the towns the ANZACs fought to save.' The Australians did save some French towns from the German offensive in 1918, but this was the exception. By the time Bullecourt and Passchendaele had been 'saved', not one brick stood on another. In any event, many of the Dutch-speaking Flemish majority in Belgium supported the German occupation. It was, they believed, an opportunity to win Flemish autonomy.

So, why were we fighting?

Because of subsequent history, Germany has come to be seen as a 'natural' enemy. But in 1914 there was nothing inevitable about Britain fighting against Germany. If Britain had a traditional enemy in Europe, it was France. Germany was a constitutional monarchy, like Britain: indeed, the two royal families were related by marriage. But after the assassination of Archduke Franz Ferdinand, the heir to the Austro-Hungarian throne, a complex series of alliances and guarantees and threats and responses to threats pulled nation after nation over the brink.

The British Empire stumbled into a war which had no clear goal and for which it was appallingly ill-prepared. Britain's strength was its navy, and this was primarily a land war. Its regular army was small and poorly equipped. Britain needed the help of the rest of the Empire. So it was that young men from almost every corner of the globe found themselves in Europe, fighting a war which was unlike anything in the human experience.

Germany's attempt to swiftly defeat France by attacking through Belgium had failed in the first two months of the war.

The generals who had planned for the Great War had imagined quick movement, rapid and decisive battles. They had not anticipated that two modern inventions, barbed wire and the machine gun, would give a decisive advantage to soldiers defending a position. Germany's attempt to swiftly defeat France by attacking through Belgium had failed in the first two months of the war. The opposing armies had built long lines of trenches and fortifications, stretching from the Belgian coast to the Swiss Alps. New technologies, such as tanks, were being developed to help the attacker but until the very end of the war these were experimental and ineffective.

In the meantime, infantry trying to attack machine guns protected by barbed wire died in waves.

In 1916, the British and French armies launched a massive assault on the German lines, on either side of the Somme River. The plan was to use massed artillery to annihilate the German defences, to break through quickly and end the war. The offensive was a catastrophe. On the first day alone, 1 July, the British took almost 60 000 casualties—19 000 of them were killed. Despite the appalling losses, the attack continued—not just for days, but for weeks and months until finally, in November, the onset of winter made any further fighting impossible.

The Somme was the bloodiest battle in human history—the combined casualties numbered more than one million. The French and British attackers advanced their positions, on average, about 7 kilometres—less than half as far as had been planned for the first day.

The Australians, who had been arriving in Europe since the failure of the Gallipoli campaign, were not involved in the first day of the Somme offensive. However, they learned the full horror of the Western Front soon enough. In conditions far worse than at Gallipoli, the Australians fought battles named after tiny hamlets long blasted out of existence: Fromelles, where they suffered 5500 casualties in twenty-four hours; Pozieres; Flers; Moquet Farm. 'The Australian attacks in 1916', military historian Jeffrey Grey writes, 'like the offensives of which they were part, were failures'. The AIF was engaged on the Somme for forty-five days and suffered some

23 000 casualties—more than twice the total of the whole Gallipoli campaign.

THE LITTLE DIGGER

Another Australian arrived in Europe in 1916: Prime Minister William Morris Hughes. 'Billy' Hughes was an unlikely leader: short, ugly, wiry, a veteran of the union movement, a politician of street-fighting instincts. He was known as a raw but effective orator. Hughes had been attorney-general in Andrew Fisher's Labor government, which came to power shortly after war broke out. In October 1915, Fisher resigned due to ill health, and Hughes was chosen as prime minister. He would hold this office for seven turbulent years.

April 1916 was a grim time in Britain. The government was divided, the war effort fumbling; people were casting about for leadership and inspiration. Into this scene stepped Hughes. Like a shop steward invited to address the board of directors, his rasping and belligerent oratory was startling and effective. He became a sensation: his strident imperialist patriotism, his demand for action, energy and ruthlessness in the prosecution of the war—they were what the audiences of the hour needed to hear.

It is hard now to understand the fuss, but Hughes was hailed as the saviour of the British Empire—it was seriously suggested he be appointed prime minister of Britain. Hughes visited the Australian troops in Britain and France, and he became—there is no other word for it—besotted. He wrote to a colleague from Paris:

> Just arrived here after a flash light tour along the Front. It is a great sight! Soldiers everywhere: great men women working everywhere: great women fit mothers of heroes: France and the world's salvation!: I inspected our fellows: What a glorious and inspiring sight they were: Fit: !Magnificent physique: Sublimely confident and cheerful.

Who knows what underlay this almost homoerotic fervour, but Hughes was sincere in his love for the 'diggers'. However, he had a funny way of showing it.

He left Britain before the disaster of the Somme started, but by the time he reached Australia the magnitude of the slaughter was obvious. Hughes response was to allow the AIF to continue under the same commanders, pursuing the same tactics and strategy, without the slightest protest. Not only that, but he wanted to send more young Australian men to be killed.

Hughes declared that Australia had to contribute more troops to the war effort, and that only conscription could supply them. He probably had the power to introduce conscription by regulation but, unsure of Senate support and confident of an overwhelming mandate, he announced that a referendum would be held in October 1916. This referendum was not an exercise in democracy. Having asked people for their opinion, Hughes launched a strident and vindictive campaign to make sure they gave the right answer.

It is difficult to convey fully the bitterness with which the conscription debate was waged in Australia. The rhetoric of radical opponents of conscription was inflammatory, but that is to be expected from radicals. The real surprises were the excesses of those at the centre of power and authority, especially Hughes. He appeared in a film appealing for a 'yes' vote, screened in cinemas around the country. A less statesmanlike address to a nation at war would be difficult to imagine. Hughes proclaimed:

> Every citizen must decide in which camp he will stand: for or against Australia, for or against Great Britain, for or against the Empire ... I warn you to beware the enemies in our midst, the agents of treacherous Germany ... To vote NO would be to abandon those gallant Australian troops who are fighting so heroically for you ... Are you going to scab on the Anzacs? ... Those who vote NO will make the Australian Commonwealth the first blackleg nation among the Allies ... If you vote 'No', spell it 'Nein'. That is how the Kaiser would spell it.

The referendum on conscription was narrowly lost. In 1917, Hughes tried again. He declared that he would resign as prime minister if he were not granted the power to conscript. Again the referendum was lost. Hughes changed his mind about resigning. The number of voluntary recruits fell away, and by 1918 many Australian units were understrength. But far more serious was the harm done to the fabric of Australian society. At every level, the institutions of civil society—from trade unions to churches, from shire councils to sporting clubs—were pulled into a welter of bitterness and recrimination.

Hughes' own Labor Party was all but destroyed—it did not really recover federally until the 1940s. Hughes walked out on Labor and formed the Nationalist Party. But this was not a conservative party in any worthwhile sense. It had no coherent philosophy or program. Its members were mostly veterans of anti-labour politics, who neither liked nor trusted Hughes.

While Hughes was indulging in his divisive campaign to get more young Australians to Europe, he made little effort to gain any influence over the fate of those already there. There was, it is true, successful pressure to have Australian units serve under Australian officers, with John Monash eventually taking overall command of the AIF. But the decisions that really mattered were made by the Imperial War Cabinet in London, and by the high command of the British Army. And it was among this handful of people that the fates of tens of thousands of Australians were decided. Here, Australia had no voice.

It was not that Australia was excluded. Hughes had been invited, even pressured, to attend an Imperial War conference in 1917. This was an attempt to settle what the Empire's war aims were, how the war should be prosecuted, what would be acceptable terms for peace. Hughes, however, declined to go. He was facing a general election and felt that he was 'indispensable' at home. Australia was unrepresented as the Empire groped for a way to end the war.

+ + +

Within the British and French governments, there was widespread confusion, exhaustion and desperation. What should be the war strategy for 1917? An amphibious landing on the Belgian coast to outflank the Germans? Helping the Italians to attack Austria? Just defending the Western Front and waiting for the United States to enter the war? Maybe even negotiated peace? The only thing that seemed to unite the advocates of a new approach was their agreement that there should not be 'another Somme'.

Amid the bickering and confusion, one man felt he knew exactly what to do: the commander in chief of the British armed forces on the Western Front, Sir Douglas Haig.

In order to fully understand the disaster that was the Flanders offensive of 1917, it is necessary to understand Haig. The whole thing was his idea. He insisted the offensive be launched despite strong opposition, including from the British prime minister, David Lloyd George. And long after its failure was obvious, Haig persisted with the attack over the repeated protests of many, including his usually sycophantic inner circle.

> **Haig persisted with the attack over the repeated protests of many, including his usually sycophantic inner circle.**

An official photograph of Haig shows him sitting at his desk, neat and businesslike. Without the military uniform, he might be some upright but dull man in middle age: the director of a building society, perhaps. But the eyes are disturbing: steely, and as cold as Flanders sleet. Haig was vain, arrogant and prone to self-delusion, as are so many military leaders. But these flaws were married with calmness, astonishing patience, resilience and an invincible sense of Christian rectitude. It is this combination—bland, unflappable competence and piety mixed with a near-total lack of human feeling—which made Haig one of the most repellent personalities in military history.

Haig was convinced that to win the war, the German Army had to be defeated through frontal assault where it was strongest—on the Western Front. He rejected any attempt to try something different, such as searching for a weak spot, as a 'sideshow', a 'distraction' from the main theatre of war. He dismissed any suggestion that it might be prudent to go on the defensive as 'pessimism'. He also rejected, utterly and with venom, any suggestion of a negotiated peace: that was 'intolerable' political interference.

It was Haig who had planned and led the Somme offensive. On the eve of battle, he wrote to his wife: '*I do feel* that in my plans I have been helped by a Power that is not my own'. This conviction that he was doing God's work, that he had not erred in any way, was to survive any setback, any catastrophe. The failure of the initial attack and the resulting slaughter prompted this note in Haig's diary: 'A day of downs and ups!' He comforted himself about the staggering casualties: 'This cannot be considered severe in view of the numbers engaged'.

To some extent, Haig can be forgiven the failure of the initial offensive on the Somme. He had planned the attack as well as he could, and honestly believed it would succeed. Events proved that terrible mistakes had been made. In particular, the artillery bombardment had not been nearly as effective as was hoped. The shelling had not destroyed the German barbed wire, nor had enemy casualties been great. Several minutes had elapsed between the end of the British barrage and the troops going over the top, so German soldiers had had ample time to leave their dugouts and set up machine guns. In addition, the attack had taken place in daylight, just after 7 a.m. As the British soldiers had advanced, in most areas walking uphill—having been ordered not to run—they had been completely exposed. One regiment, from Newfoundland, had suffered 90 per cent casualties in less than half an hour.

But Haig was oblivious to the lack of success. The breakthrough which had been planned was quietly forgotten and vague, ever-shifting goals were adopted. Day after bloody, fatal day, he would write in his diary.

> The battle is developing slowly but steadily in our favour ... The battle is being fought on lines which suit us ... This is indeed a very great success ... captured this morning several important trenches ... The success has come at a most opportune moment.

This last entry was written a few days before winter set in and operations had to be abandoned. By this time, the French and British armies had suffered 794 000 casualties and captured a few square kilometres of blasted mud. Haig was satisfied. The British Empire, he believed, had proven its fighting qualities, and only bad weather had prevented total success. The thing to do—the *only* thing to do—was to continue attacking the following year, as soon as the weather was good enough.

The British prime minister despised Haig and thought that the whole Somme offensive had been murderous folly. He tried to manoeuvre Haig into resigning, but did not

> **Steadfast, determined, resolute, Haig pushed for his plan, an offensive north of the Somme, in Flanders. He saw, with complete clarity, what should be done.**

feel politically secure enough to sack a man who was a close personal friend of King George V.

Determined and resolute, Haig pushed for his plan, an offensive north of the Somme, in Flanders. He saw, with complete clarity, what should be done. As the governments of Britain and France bickered and prevaricated, he noted in his diary:

> 1. Send to France every possible man
> 2. "   "   "   "   "   aeroplane
> 3. "   "   "   "   "   gun

Because there was no real agreement among his many opponents about an alternative plan, and because he was willing to defy his prime minister, Haig eventually got his way.

BULLECOURT

In April 1917, a badly planned attack by the French Army was launched at Aisne. It was a shocking failure, with more than 100 000 casualties suffered in the first few days. The fiasco caused a mutiny which spread through much of the army. Meanwhile, to support the French, the British attacked further north, at Arras. As an offshoot of this operation the 3rd Division, AIF, was to make a diversion by attacking near the small French village of Bullecourt. It was, in the context of the war, a minor affair, a diversion for an offensive which was itself a diversion. It rates scarcely a paragraph in most histories. But it exemplified the madness of much of the 1917 campaign, and set the tone for what was to come.

From the beginning, the Bullecourt plan was deeply flawed. The attack was aimed at the fortified village of Reincourt. To reach it, the Australians had to pass between two German strong points: Bullecourt, to the left, and Queant, to the right. Both were fortified with barbed wire and with machine guns in concrete blockhouses. In military jargon, this was called a 'double re-entrant'. As they advanced, the Australians would be exposed to fire on both sides as well as from the front. By the time they reached the German wire, they could be fired on from behind as well.

The bitter lesson of the war so far was that infantry could not attack well-defended positions except with overwhelming artillery support. Because of transport difficulties, there was little ammunition for the artillery to provide cover for the Australians. This should have ended all thoughts of an attack. But instead it was proposed that the infantry would be supported by tanks.

First used at the Somme the previous year, these steel-plated behemoths were terrifying in their size and noise. Armed with cannons and machine guns, lumbering along on caterpillar tracks, they could cross the butchered ground of no-man's-land and crush barbed-wire entanglements, leaving a clear path for infantry. Tanks promised a way to break the deadlock on the Western Front, and eventually they would deliver on this promise. But in 1917 they were still experimental weapons. They were slow, only able to move at 3 or 4 kilometres per hour. They were unreliable, frequently breaking down. They were so heavy, weighing some 30 tonnes, that in muddy conditions they were likely to get bogged, and they were vulnerable to shell fire. It was also hard to maintain the element of surprise, as the tanks made so much noise that they could be heard from several kilometres away.

But the commanders of the Tank Corps promised wonderful results, and the generals were only too willing to believe. And so it was that the Anzacs were sent to attack the German line at Bullecourt with no artillery barrage—the tanks would clear the way. The raid was planned to take place before dawn on 10 April, but by 5 a.m. the tanks had not arrived. The operation was cancelled and the Australian troops, who were out at their 'jumping off' positions, had to retreat before they were exposed by daylight.

Over the objections of the Australian command, Haig ordered the attack to take place the following day. Again, the tanks did not arrive in time. But the Australian troops were ordered to proceed regardless. Light snow had fallen, which meant that the dark shapes of the soldiers stood out clearly against the ground.

At 5 a.m., the waiting Australians were detected. German fire was so intense that the barbed wire, as one Australian officer put it, 'seemed to swarm with fireflies' as glancing bullets threw up sparks. At this dire moment, Major Percy Black, a popular and courageous officer from Western Australia, moved forward to the first line of his men and shouted: 'Come on boys, bugger the tanks'. Under fire from both sides, the Australians advanced, struggling through whatever gaps in the barbed wire they could find. They captured the first German trench and pushed on to the second trench, despite Black being killed.

A section of the second trench was then captured, but by 6 a.m. it was daylight. The Australians were cut off, machine guns sweeping the ground behind them as well as in front. They were forced to surrender—more than 1100 were captured—or to retreat though heavy fire. Many of the wounded were left stranded among the barbed wire.

The Australians suffered more than 3000 casualties at Bullecourt—the 4th Brigade alone lost 2339 of its 3000 men. It was a disaster, but none of the commanders responsible was dismissed, or even reprimanded. In his diary, Haig described the action as a modest success.

There is a tendency in Australian accounts of events such as those at Bullecourt to slip into nationalism, praising Aussie courage and deriding 'blundering British generals'. This view misunderstands the political and emotional world of the Great War. We were all 'British', it didn't matter whether we were born in Canada, South Africa, New Zealand or Scotland; we were privileged to be part of the greatest Empire the world had known. There were, it was true, a great many people who were excluded. It was a little unclear just what the 'British race' was. But it most certainly was white. To some extent 'British' meant Protestant, too—understandably a source of resentment among Catholics.

For all that, the concept of being 'British' had genuine meaning, and Australia was part of the club. And the Empire was open to its constituent members. The British prime minister, David Lloyd George, was a Welshman. Sir Douglas

Haig was a Scot. And Haig, for his part, didn't discriminate between subjects of the Empire. He sent English factory hands and Welsh pit boys and crofters from his native land to be slaughtered with just as little concern as he showed for colonial units.

THE DEADLY SALIENT

After the failure of Arras, and while the AIF regrouped and tried to restore numbers and morale, Haig pushed on with his great plan. The British Empire—alone now, with mutiny crippling the French Army—would attack in Flanders, breaking through the German line and forcing the German Army to stand and fight, and to be destroyed. The place of attack was the salient projecting north-east of the ruined Flemish town of Ypres.

A salient is a bulge or projection in a line. The term came into military usage to describe a strong point, like a tower projecting from a fortress. In the Great War, however, the term took on a new meaning. In trench warfare, a salient was often a weak spot. This was especially true if the bulge in the line was not on high ground. A salient which lay in a valley, surrounded by hills, was a death trap.

And that is what the Ypres salient was. The British had managed to halt the German advance there in 1914 and had held it ever since, taking almost constant losses because the position was so exposed. By 1917, millions of men had lived and fought in the salient, and many had died there. Like much of Flanders—the name means 'flooded land'—the country was reclaimed swamp. With drainage systems destroyed by shelling, the salient became waterlogged. The corpses of men and pack animals mixed with the detritus of war such as poison gas, petrol and explosives, making a toxic brew of the ground water which oozed constantly into the trenches where the soldiers sheltered.

To get across the ground, soldiers had to walk on wooden planking, 'duckboards', laid across the mud. The plank roads threaded slightly firmer ground between shell holes full of slime and rotting corpses, and it was on these roads that the Germans concentrated their fire. The men who shuffled towards the front line, or staggered back carrying the wounded on stretchers, suffered a dual terror. There was death from shrapnel and high explosive, but even worse was slipping into the slime and drowning: men who were sinking and could not be reached would beg to be shot.

This was the battlefield into which Haig sent the armies of the British Empire, including the Australians—a stinking wasteland, foul with shit and death and poison.

On the eve of the Ypres offensive, in August, Pope Benedict XV broke the great taboo. He publicly appealed to the combatant nations to stop the slaughter: 'Shall, then, the civilised world be naught but a field of death? And shall Europe ... lend her hand to her own suicide?' He proposed, as a basis for beginning negotiations, a return to prewar territorial boundaries.

Billy Hughes was among the most strident in denouncing the very suggestion, as Australia would then have to hand back control of German New Guinea, seized early in the war. As for Haig, he confided to his diary: 'My chief fear is that Germany might offer in October or November terms of peace which the Allied governments might accept'. Haig wanted his great offensive, the push in Flanders, 'the decisive point', by which 'final victory may be won by December'.

The first phase of the offensive had already taken place: the capture of high ground to the south of Ypres, at Messines. On 7 June 1917, several huge mines dug under the German line were exploded simultaneously. British troops, including the Australians, advanced and held the captured territory in the face of powerful counterattacks. The assault was conducted under the philosophy of the limited objective, a reaction to the disaster of the Somme: after careful planning troops would attack with massive artillery support, reach clear, defined and achievable goals, and then stop.

Messines was considered a brilliant success, a triumph of the new approach, and caused a huge lift in the morale of British troops. It was the sort of 'victory', though, which could be seen as such only by the desolate standards of the Western Front. The British had moved forward several thousand metres and stayed there. But the cost was enormous: 26 000 casualties, more than half of whom were Australians.

The 'triumph' of Messines was only a prelude to the main offensive in the Ypres salient. Because Ypres was under the eyes of the Germans, it was perfectly obvious to them what was coming. As the men, guns and supplies were assembled in the back areas, the Germans were able to shell them with devastating impact.

Before the main attack, Haig wanted to 'even out' the front line to facilitate a breakthrough. The grim result is summarised by the Australian official war historian CEW Bean: 'one local attack after another, delivered in dreadful conditions of mud, on narrow fronts, against the concentrated fire of the enemy's available artillery'. These efforts to capture some higher ground were almost total failures. In little more than a month, the British lost 109 000 men, with almost nothing to show for it.

On 20 September, a major attack was launched at Menin Road. A well-planned artillery barrage supported the troops, who made a defined and limited advance. The 1st and 2nd Australian divisions were in the thick of the fighting and acquitted themselves well. It was, Bean wrote, 'a complete success'. Again, that depends on what you call success. The British forces lost about 23 000 men, 5000 of them Australian.

The British continued to press on slowly towards the ridges surrounding the salient. They captured Polygon Wood, a place as small as its name suggests and which had scarcely a tree standing. One Australian wrote of this action: 'My God, it was terrible. Just slaughter. The 5th Div. were almost annihilated. We certainly gained our objectives, but what a cost'.

The hamlet of Broodseinde was attacked in October. It was seen as a smashing victory. Bean thought the Australians 'had never fought better' and that 'an overwhelming blow had been struck'. But again, this was a bitter victory, with 5600 Australian casualties.

The success of Broodseinde inspired Haig in his belief that a decisive breakthrough was possible. He told his commanders 'we must be prepared to exploit our successful attack and so achieve more decisive results'. In other words, forget limited objectives.

Troops were brought in from other sectors and the cavalry placed on standby to exploit the breakthrough, even though thousands of horses had drowned in the mud of the salient. The focus of the decisive attack was to be a little village on a low ridge: Passchendaele.

Then the weather broke. On 5 October it began to rain heavily, and a few days later torrential rain set in. On the battlefield, there was paralysis. The wounded could not be evacuated. There was no shelter for them at the front—if they were placed in a shell hole or a trench, they might drown. So they lay in the open, exposed to the rain and to shelling.

It became impossible to move artillery: pack animals would sink up to their necks in the bog. Ammunition, carried over the duckboards by mules and even on the backs of men, was often coated in mud and unusable. Even if guns could be brought into position, it was hard to find ground solid enough to fire from, and almost impossible to fire accurately. The 'march' to the front line was an exhausting struggle. The 66th Anzac Division, called up to take part in the attack on Passchendaele, took ten hours to cover less than 6 kilometres.

Haig's reaction to the appalling conditions? Following his own private, insane logic, he decided to attack earlier than had been planned. Even his closest supporters, including the most senior generals, opposed him. But on 9 October, in pelting rain, the assault went ahead.

The soldiers struggled through the mud and barbed wire towards Passchendaele and were cut down by the German machine guns. Attempts to destroy German strong points by rushing them sometimes succeeded, but at a hideous cost. In one such action, a raiding party of eighty-five returned with only fourteen survivors. By evening, the Australians had taken heavy casualties and were still well short of their first objective.

The response of the command was surreal. Haig noted in his diary 'the results were very successful … the 66th Division advanced without barrage and took all objectives'.

The soldiers at the front line were exhausted and demoralised. Because of the contaminated groundwater, the ingestion of which could not be avoided, many troops were weakened by dysentery. It was impossible to construct any sort of shelter, or to get dry. It was also difficult to secure any sort of protection from the constant shelling. 'The idea of "digging in" was ridiculous', one survivor recalled. 'You can't dig water!'

Haig told the press : 'It was simply the mud that defeated us on Tuesday. The men did splendidly [to] get through it as they did'. He still hoped for a breakthrough, and added a further objective—the village of Passchendaele itself. Once this was taken, 'the rest of the ridge would fall more easily'.

Again, Haig's generals tried to abandon the attack. Again, they were overruled, despite very few guns being able to fire on the German lines.

On 11 October, the 3rd Australian Division set out to capture Passchendaele. The New Zealand Division was supposed to support them by capturing a German strong point, but it was impossible. The New Zealanders had to cross a valley, the mud waist-deep in most places, and face uncut barbed wire and heavy fire. They were slaughtered. 'Everyone', a survivor recalled, 'was either scattered, wounded, or dead'.

The failure of the New Zealand attack left the Australians even more exposed. Astonishingly, some Australians did reach their objectives—a small party even got through to Passchendaele—but they were isolated, exhausted and under constant fire.

On 13 October, the Australians were ordered to retire to the line they had held two days before. An Australian officer described the scene:

> The slope ... was littered with dead, both theirs and ours. I got to one pill box to find it just a mass of dead [further on] I found about fifty men alive ... never have I seen men so broken or demoralised. They were huddled up close behind the [pill box] in the last stages of exhaustion and fear. Fritz had been sniping them off all day ... the dead and dying lay in piles. The wounded were numerous—unattended and weak ... The stench was dreadful.

The Australians had lost 4200 men and the New Zealanders another 1000. The failure of the attack persuaded

Haig that there was no possibility of breaking through. He returned to the philosophy of limited objectives, and decided to attack ... Passchendaele.

This time it was the Canadians who led the assault, with Australian support. Among the support units was the 8th Battalion, 2nd Brigade, AIF, in which served Thomas William James Mehegan, of Preston, Victoria. He had already been wounded in action in May, but had returned to his unit and been promoted to corporal. On 25 October he was killed in action.

The Canadians attacked on 26 October, but had no more success than the Australians. Haig declared: 'The positions won by the Canadians today ... are of the greatest importance ... I was entirely opposed to abandoning the operations'. The Canadians tried again, and on 6 November finally captured Passchendaele. Haig regarded the capture of the village, or what was left of it, as 'a very important success'.

And so the Flanders offensive finally came to an end. It had achieved none of its original objectives. At its furthest point, the front line had advanced 8 kilometres. It was the equivalent of attacking south-west from the centre of Sydney, and capturing Marrickville. It had cost the British 449 000 casualties; Australia had lost 38 093 officers and men. The capture of Passchendaele was strategically pointless. The whole offensive had merely made the Ypres salient deeper, and harder to defend.

> **The front line had advanced 8 kilometres. It was the equivalent of attacking south-west from the centre of Sydney, and capturing Marrickville.**

'FOR KING AND EMPIRE'

The following spring, the German Army mounted a massive offensive in France. The Allies were taken completely by surprise. The German Army smashed through the front line, causing panic and headlong retreat. For a time, it was feared that Paris might fall. But in April, under the leadership of General John Monash, the Australian Army halted the German push at Amiens. Then, in August, using new tactics that combined careful planning and supporting troops with tanks, aeroplanes and artillery, the AIF broke through the German lines. By November, facing mutiny in the armed forces and civic collapse, Germany sued for peace. An armistice was signed, and on 11 November the guns fell silent.

Billy Hughes was furious—he had not been consulted about the peace terms. Haig was pleased, but not for long. In the victory parade to be held in London, he was to ride in the fifth carriage, and worse, with the French commander General Foch. Haig, so unflappable in sending hundreds of thousands of soldiers to their deaths, threw a temper tantrum. 'Was there ever such an insult prepared for the welcome of a General on his return', he railed. It was 'more of an insult than I could put up with, even from the Prime Minister'.

The AIF's achievements in France in 1918 were and remain worth honouring. But they should not obscure the magnitude of the debacle of Flanders. Indeed, the events of 1918 only underscore how appalling were the decisions made the previous year. In the face of the German offensive further south, the British quietly did what they should always have done and abandoned the Ypres salient, surrendering a few miles of strategically unimportant countryside to take up more easily defended positions.

What good can be extracted from the mud of Passchendaele? From a humanitarian point of view, nothing. From an Australian point of view, our soldiers had, most of the time, fought well. There were incidents of indiscipline and what was called cowardice, though succumbing to terror is perhaps a better description. There were, it is beyond denial, occasions when Australians murdered enemy soldiers who had surrendered. But on the whole, the men of the AIF had proven themselves brave, skilful and adaptable.

After the war, General Monash attributed the remarkable fighting qualities of the Australian soldier to:

> The democratic institutions under which he was reared, the advanced system of education by which he was trained— teaching him to think for himself and to apply what he had been taught to practical ends ... mentally the Australian soldier was well endowed. In him there was a curious blend of capacity for independent judgement with a readiness to submit to self-effacement in a common cause.

But what was this cause?

In 1916, Hughes said that the Great War was being fought so that 'we will emerge triumphant, with our great Empire welded indissolubly together'. It is a common mistake to call the AIF the Australian Infantry Force. This is almost a Freudian slip: it was the Australian *Imperial* Force. As the scroll over the Preston war memorial says, those who served did so 'for King and Empire'.

But if the Empire is what we fought for, then it was all a tragic waste. On the killing grounds of the Western Front, where Douglas Haig spilled the blood of the Empire's sons and emptied its treasuries, the British Empire took a mortal blow. Its long, slow death was not obvious for another quarter of a century, during another war. It was the fall of Singapore in February 1942 that marked the end of the Empire for Australia and a seismic shift in our world view.

It was the fall of Singapore in February 1942 that marked the end of the Empire for Australia and a seismic shift in our world view.

The disaster of the Great War, however, could be denied. We had, after all, won. Defeat lays things bare; victory can hide a multitude of sins. Superficially, the political structure of the Empire remained in place for another thirty years.

Not only was denial possible, it was *necessary*. If such sacrifice for the Empire had been for nothing, then ... no, that was too awful to contemplate. The Great War left Australia exhausted, divided and in debt. The confident, vigorous nation that had come together at Federation retreated into protectionist isolationism, bereft of ideas and energy, scarred by a deep trauma.

When the war broke out, the opposition leader, Andrew Fisher, declared that the nation would fight 'to the last man and the last shilling'. Australia very nearly did so. By the end of the war, 417 000 Australians had enlisted in the armed forces—this from a population of four million. The cost of supporting this large army was staggering: £377 million was spent, £263 million of which was borrowed. The nation's entire export income for 1914–15 was less than £63 million.

Of those who enlisted, 80 per cent served overseas, mostly in France and Belgium. It was mostly in France and Belgium, too, that the 59 000 who were killed lost their lives. Another 4000 went missing and were never accounted for. This represented almost one in ten Australian men of military age. There were 167 000 battle casualties, and another 88 000 men suffered serious illness. Perhaps 60 000 of those injured in the war died prematurely, through illness or by their own hands. Many others were permanently incapacitated. As historian Geoffrey Blainey put it, these were the future poets and politicians, union leaders and journalists, doctors and judges, teachers and priests, husbands and fathers of Australia. So many of them died.

The disaster of the Western Front was, in some ways, harder for Australians to assimilate than for Europeans. The horror of the battlefield was on the far side of the world, remote and incomprehensible to those who had stayed behind. Those who loved the men who marched away, and did not return, did not even have a body to bury. After peace was declared, the Ypres salient became a place of pilgrimage, where family members sought out and honoured the graves of their loved ones. The emotional benefit of being able to visit a grave, lay a wreath, say a prayer, was immense.

Very few Australians could make this journey. How to mourn when there is no body, no funeral, and your loss is spoken of in arid abstractions: sacrifice, duty, glory? The answer is in those thousands of marble columns and granite pillars and bronze statues of solemn diggers, with their rows and rows of names. Australia's war memorials are gravestones for those whose graves are far away. They are the dignified public expression of terrible private grief—'He died in France!'—a way for a people not given to expressing emotion to weep for its lost children.

Many of those soldiers who did return did so as broken men. Their misery and pain rippled out through society, scarring their families and friends. The hurt robbed children of loving fathers, setting up cycles of alcoholism and abuse which rolled through generations.

Those who returned did not, for the most part, want to talk about their experiences. And most of those who had not experienced the war did not want to know. The reactions of Australians to attempts at recording the emotional truth of the Great War were telling. Robert Graves, the British poet and novelist, wrote a vivid and compelling memoir of the war, *Goodbye to All That*. Graves mentioned that Australian troops had a bad reputation for killing German prisoners, which was true. But there was outrage here, and the book was banned. Jean Remarque's novel about the German experience of the war, *All Quiet on the Western Front*, was also banned for being 'pro-German'. An Australian, Frederic Manning, wrote *Her Privates We*, one of the very few pieces of quality literature to emerge from the Australian experience of the war. Its publication aroused fury, especially for its 'indecency', and it was banned in Australia.

The reasons expressed for banning these and other works differed, but the underlying rationale was always denial. The Anzacs were heroes, the war saved the Empire, and the sacrifice of the soldiers lifted Australia to glory.

In place of the raw, shocking and varied truth of human experience, the mythology of the digger was constructed. There was, of course, some truth in the stories of humour and ingenuity and cheerful courage under fire, the insubordinate streak of the Australian soldier. But chewed upon over and over, these became a stale, inward-looking and uncritical myth.

This myth fossilised into a damaging complacency, a sterile rhetoric used to obscure any need for criticism, analysis or reform. The Australian soldier becomes beyond criticism, a semi-sacred figure. And if the digger can do no wrong, the armed forces can escape scrutiny and accountability, allowing waste and malpractice to go unchecked.

Australian histories of World War I tend to fall into one of two groups. Military histories are usually fairly conservative and focus on the success or failure of this or that offensive. There are even some that continue to defend Haig as 'the soldier who ensured Allied victory'. When a scene of carnage is particularly indefensible, something is salvaged by admiring the courage and sacrifice of the troops.

More critical histories tend to focus on the human suffering in the trenches, or on the politics of the home front, and ignore military and political decision-making. The whole thing was, after all, a sham.

Both approaches are inadequate. It is possible to accept the political, social and cultural worldview of the time and still recognise that what happened on the Western Front in 1916 and 1917 was a disaster.

The 'democratic institutions' of which Monash was so proud failed during the Great War. The democratically elected governments of the British Empire lost control of their own armed forces. The institutions of civic society in Australia, including political parties and parliaments, failed to control an executive government dominated by one man.

Under Hughes' leadership, the most reckless, bloody-minded and idiotic decisions of the military machine were cheered on by Australia, and paid for with Australian blood.

The Great War changed Australia, and not for the better. In its wake, Australians denied what the war really meant. To a great extent, we continue to deny it to this day. Each Anzac Day, when we prattle on about mateship and avoid awkward questions about what exactly we were fighting for, the denial continues.

Australia's forests and heaths once supported abundant species of large marsupials. Their extinction was the continent's first great disaster. (Photograph by Denise McDonald 2008)

3
DESTROYING THE PROMISED LAND: THE GREAT RESOURCE CRASH, c. 40 000 BC

We don't have mountains in Australia. I had thought we did, and then I went to New Zealand and saw Mt Cook—soaring up, up, up; snow on the peak in high summer; jagged, sharp-edged —and realised that in Australia we have hills.

We don't have rivers, either. People sometimes speak of the 'mighty' Murray River. They should fly into Shanghai and look out the window as the aeroplane passes over the Yangtze, a vast, slow-moving inland sea, kilometres wide, thick with boat traffic.

Something else we don't have is soil. On the loess plains of China, what we call 'topsoil' is metres deep. In places, the farmers dig square pits the size of soccer fields and perhaps 4 metres deep, and plant orchards at the bottom. The fruit trees are sheltered from the wind and grow happily, with many more metres of rich soil beneath them. It is a startling sight to anyone used to Australia, where soil is such a precious resource, thin and fragile, with the bones of the land poking through.

Australia is old, even in the epochal stretches of time which geologists so calmly use to measure the history of the earth. There are rocks in the deserts of Western Australia which were formed 3.6 billion years ago—the planet itself is not much older. That it is the driest continent apart from Antarctica is well known. It is also, without exception, the flattest.

It has another distinction. A satellite picture of the earth at night, a composite amassed from a year of images, shows Australia to be relatively empty, the points of light cast by cities and towns thinner than in Europe or Asia. But there is a smudge of brightness across almost the whole continent, even the inland deserts: light from bushfires and grassfires. Australia is a dry land, a land of poor soil, and a land of fire. This is partly due to forces of nature, but it is also due to human actions.

From the time of its separation from the supercontinent Gondwana some 80 million years ago, Australia has ridden on the middle of its tectonic plate, little troubled by the massive forces that can raise mountain ranges and volcanoes. It is these forces which bring mineral nutrients to the surface of the earth, and fertility and renewed life to the landscape. And so, for aeons, Australia has been in the grip of entropy, a slow winding down. Isolated from other continents, Australia's plants and animals have evolved and adapted to life in a giant Noah's ark that has been running low on supplies.

The ancient rainforests of Gondwana dwindled as Australia moved north and the climate became hotter and drier. Tiny pockets survived—here and there they still do—but the dominant vegetation became what fire historian Stephen Pyne calls the scleroforest. 'Sclero' is derived from the Greek word for 'hard'. The trees of the scleroforest have tough, small leaves that conserve moisture, and woody fruits, and are able to endure, even thrive, in arid seasons.

Living in this dry Eden were many different species of marsupial. Some were very similar to the kangaroos and wombats and possums we know today; others were 'megafauna': giant kangaroos and echidnas, and a relative of the wombat as large as a rhino. There were also marsupial predators, some as large as lions, which preyed on the plant eaters.

Some of these species were already under pressure some 40 000 years ago. The world was in the grip of an ice age, and Australia had become both colder and drier. But then a new group of deadly predators arrived—not physically powerful, but with large brains and a knowledge of tools. The most potent of these tools was fire.

> **When humans first arrived on the Australian continent more than 45 000 years ago, there were abundant species of megafauna. They must have seemed like gifts from the gods.**

To understand the Australian environment, and the place of humans in it, it is necessary to forget the idea of wilderness. When we talk of 'nature' or 'the environment', we tend to think of something like a well-managed national park. Words like 'pristine' and 'untouched' all stem from this notion, that of a stable state of pure nature, free from human impacts. But the whole Australian continent has been inhabited since long before the last ice age.

When humans first arrived on the Australian continent more than 45 000 years ago, the abundant species of megafauna must have seemed like gifts from the gods. They were ideal game for hunters and gatherers: an excellent source of food, their hides and bones and sinews useful for making tools and clothing. Most of the megafauna had small brains and, never having encountered humans before, may not have recognised them as predators. They were, in other words, stupid and easy to kill.

In a relatively short space of time, the megafauna disappeared. The timing of these extinctions is not known with exactness, and it varied between species, but by about 40 000 years ago, the big animals were gone. It is possible that these mass extinctions were due to changes in climate or other factors. But the bulk of recent research supports the conclusion that humans were the ultimate cause. The animals that survived were fast movers, like emus and kangaroos, or able to hide in the trees or in burrows, like koalas and wombats. This suggests that the extinctions were caused by a predator, and the only new predator over this time was Homo sapiens.

We exterminated some animals by over-exploiting them, while driving others, such as large carnivores, to extinction by outcompeting them. The use of fire also had a big impact.

The scleroforest had long lived with fire, caused mostly by lighting strikes. But human fire occurred more frequently and was more extensive, and it changed the landscape. Stephen Pyne argues that Aboriginal people used fire to manage the land and shape the environment for their own benefit, keeping woodlands clear and promoting regrowth. European explorers frequently remarked on the large numbers of fires burning.

When the *Endeavour* came upon the east coast of Australia, James Cook described it as 'this continent of smoke'.

Fire was also a means by which nutrients—the nitrogen, phosphorous and potassium necessary for plant life—were recycled. However, compared with plant-eating animals, which return nutrients to the soil through their manure, fire has many drawbacks. In particular, it is inefficient: each time a forest burns, a lot of nutrients literally go up in smoke.

The Australian forest has adjusted to burning. Indeed, many major plants, such as the majestic mountain ash, can regenerate in no other way. There developed a three-way symbiosis between the plants which thrive on fire—especially eucalypts—humans, and fire itself. Each benefited from the other. However, looking at the broader environmental picture, the introduction of human-managed fire regimes changed the landscape so that it could no longer support giant animals. As Flannery puts it, 'fire has made Australia—originally the most resource-poor land—an even poorer land'.

The extinction of Australian megafauna is something of a delicate subject because of the uneasy politics of race in Australia. Anything which suggests that the First Australians were less than perfect custodians of the land is seized on for political ends. In reaction, Aboriginals and those sympathetic to their cause often condemn the very idea that humans wiped out the megafauna as pedalling racism.

It is not certain that the extinction of the megafauna was the result of human action. It is, however, very likely. This has no adverse implications for modern Aboriginal people. On the contrary, I see the disaster of the megafauna extinction as a symbol of human unity. We are all so alike, even in the mistakes we make.

THE UNIVERSAL DISASTER

From prehistory, the story is repeated. Humans use their intelligence and adaptability to discover new land, blessed with some rich resource. It might be grazing pastures, or a forest, or somewhere with game animals, or fish. We take advantage of the resource, which seems boundless. But by over-exploiting it, or by destroying something else on which it depends, the resource becomes scarce, perhaps disappearing entirely.

Often, we learn to live in this new, diminished environment. We survive the resource crash, learn from it, adapt. Sometimes, the result is catastrophe: entire social systems collapse, swept away by famine and disease and war.

The textbook example of resource crash disaster is Easter Island. Settled by Polynesians, those astonishing mariners who colonised almost the entire Pacific, Easter Island is extraordinarily remote. Located in a wild stretch of the southern Pacific, it is a speck of land, only 16 kilometres across at its widest, and thousands of kilometres from any other inhabited place.

The soil is fertile but arable areas are small, and fresh water is scarce. However, when it was first settled, in about 900 AD, there were forests of palms and other large trees, and plentiful birds and shellfish along the shoreline. The waters around Easter Island are too cold to support coral reefs, but islanders used ocean-going canoes to catch porpoises and deep-sea fish, such as tuna.

The shellfish were eventually over-exploited, and the larger species became very scarce. The birds and their eggs were taken for food, both by people and by the rats which arrived with them, and in time all but one species of bird became extinct on the island. But most serious was the loss of the forest. The trees were cut down for firewood and structural timber, to make canoes, and for the ropes and props necessary to erect the giant statues for which the island is famous.

Often, we learn to live in this new, diminished environment. We survive the resource crash, learn from it, adapt. Sometimes, the result is catastrophe: entire social systems collapse, swept away by famine and disease and war.

The harvest was not sustainable. Within about 500 years of the arrival of humans, the island had been completely denuded. With no wood to make large canoes, it was impossible to catch deep-water fish. The only fuel was dry grass and scraps of sugarcane. The bare land was vulnerable to erosion, reducing food crops. The disaster unfolded in grim sequence: starvation, population crash, and a desperate, violent struggle for the resources that remained.

When European sailors first came upon Easter Island in the early eighteenth century, it was a barren wasteland. At its peak, it may have supported more than 30 000 people. Captain Cook, who visited aboard the *Endeavour* in 1774, estimated the population at about 700. (The true number was probably higher.)

Because it was so remote, the tragedy of Easter Island was extreme. Its people had lost the means to leave, and no help could come from outside—when European ships did come, in the nineteenth century, they brought only further destruction through smallpox and slavery. But the pattern of colonisation, over-exploitation and resource crash is an almost universal human experience. For many societies, it is the first great disaster. It is the moment when a promised land, perhaps found after great risk and hardship, turns against the newcomers.

It also happened to the Maori people, who settled New Zealand about 1000 years ago. The islands had a unique fauna, dominated by birds, some of which had evolved to enormous size. Among them was the moa, something like a giant emu, towering up to 3 metres high and weighing 250 kilograms. The moa quickly became a staple of the Maori diet: it was easy to kill and gave plenty of meat. However, because it was such an attractive target, and did not reproduce quickly, every species of moa became extinct. The Maori were forced into painful adjustment, subsisting on foods which were far harder to obtain.

The same pattern occurred in Europe during the last ice age, where Neolithic hunters exterminated the woolly mammoth, the woolly rhinoceros and the giant elk. In the Americas, the ancestors of Native Americans hunted out many species of large animals, and the pattern was the same when Europeans arrived and all but wiped out animals such as the bison.

And European settlers did it here, in Australia. In the arrogance of the imperial age, the society which believed itself to be the acme of human development repeated the oldest of human mistakes: finding the land of plenty, and trashing it.

In the first decade of the twentieth century, a young journalist, CEW Bean—later a famous war correspondent—travelled throughout western New South Wales, observing the land and the people who lived on it. Bean's book *On the Wool Track* is an absorbing piece of social observation. It is also a lament for environmental destruction, and a cry of warning.

They overstocked the pastures and cut down the trees, and within a decade the grass was gone.

As late as the 1880s, the plains around Cobar were thick with native grasses and saltbush. The soil was thin, but as little as 20 millimetres of rain would produce luxuriant growth. Then white settlers arrived with huge flocks of sheep. They overstocked the pastures and cut down the trees, and within a decade the grass was gone. In many places the soil was gone too. There were good rains in 1891, but nothing grew.

Bean wrote:

> When the white man raw, inexperienced, ignorant, struggled out on to those apparently rich plains and proceeded to manhandle the scrub and the grass, [he destroyed] in less than twenty years much of the wealth that had been gradually stored there from the beginning of the world ... patches of this country blew away ... It is not that the desert is encroaching on its delicate border lands; it is that we are turning parts of it into desert.

ADAPTATION

The arrival of humans and fire, and the extinction of the megafauna, changed the Australian environment forever.

In turn, the resource crash was a disaster for humans. That the Aboriginal people adapted successfully to this disaster is demonstrated by their continued survival as a family of peoples, in environments ranging from temperate grasslands to tropical rainforests, from the arid heart of the continent to the chilly shores of Tasmania.

Indigenous life was hard, and sometimes cruel. The hunter-gatherer economy was not particularly productive and could support only modest populations. But it was a successful response. By learning new skills and developing intimate knowledge of the land and waters, plants and animals, and by creating cultures which preserved this knowledge, Aboriginal people were able to sustain some of the longest continual human occupations known anywhere on earth.

But as the age of European exploration unfolded, and more and more parts of the Australian continent became known to the outside world, it was inevitable that ships would come, and with them new colonisers.

The Europeans had writing and algebra, woven cloth and alcohol, guns and steel tools. But coming from a society still partly feudal, what they wanted most was land. While white settlements were small there was conflict, but it was sporadic and marginal. Tragedy built as settlement spread into country which, to the newcomers, appeared vacant, but which to Aboriginal people was as clearly marked and as steeped in tradition as any parish in Hertfordshire.

The world that Indigenous Australians had created in the wake of disaster would be tested, and often destroyed. White settlement was another great rupture, another point at which everything became different.

Tasmanian Aboriginals at Oyster Cove in the 1850s, among the few survivors of George Augustus Robinson's 'Friendly Mission'. (Archives Office of Tasmania: AB713/1/11693)

4 THE TASMANIAN GENOCIDE: 1804–1838

In *The War of the Worlds*, published in 1898, the science-fiction writer HG Wells imagined an invasion of earth by Martians. The aliens are utterly ruthless and use their superior technology to kill everyone in their path. The narrator reflects that the English, who bear the brunt of the invasion, have no cause to condemn the Martians.

> Before we judge of them too harshly we must remember what ruthless and utter destruction our own species has wrought, not only upon animals, such as the vanished bison and the dodo, but upon its inferior races. The Tasmanians, in spite of their human likeness, were entirely swept out of existence in a war of extermination waged by European immigrants, in the space of fifty years. Are we such apostles of mercy as to complain if the Martians warred in the same spirit?

Wells' casual racism reflected the dominant beliefs of his age, but his words also reflect the fact that, by the end of the nineteenth century, the British Empire had a bad conscience over the fate of the Aboriginal people of Tasmania.

The Aboriginals had survived in isolation on their remote island since the end of the last ice age 12 000 years earlier.

They had their own languages—as many as nine or ten—and an economy, religion and a social order, with interlinked clan groups spread across most of the island. The total population is unknown—estimates vary from 2000 to 6000. What is certain is that within a single generation—from the establishment of the first British penal colony in 1804 to 1838, when only about eighty-two Aboriginals survived—almost an entire people was annihilated.

When I was a teenager, a friend lent me a strange book. It was a reproduction of an old newspaper, the *Hobart Town Gazette and Southern Reporter*, a little news-sheet which chronicled life in the penal colony of Van Diemen's Land (as Tasmania was known until 1863). I became entranced, reading the notices of escaped convicts with their pitiful details—'William Jones, height: 5'1", 17 years old, marked with the pox'—advertisements for soap and candles and tea, and little items of parish pump news: the price of bread, the wheat harvest is doing well, a recipe for rat poison. This mulch of historical detail brought the past to life, in all its messy complexity.

From the establishment of the first British penal colony in 1804 to 1838 almost an entire people was annihilated.

Ever present is the iron machinery of the penal colony. In Van Diemen's Land, a person's legal status was the most important thing about them. News reports would, as a matter of course, follow a person's name with 'settler', 'free man', 'crown servant' or 'crown prisoner'.

The *Gazette* calmly recorded the varied business each week at the Hobart Magistrate's Court: John Nowland is given a licence to operate a ferry; Andrew Levy, a free man, is fined £5 for selling liquor without a licence; James Brown and William McDonald, crown prisoners, are convicted of stealing two sheep and both sentenced to 200 lashes and twelve months in irons in the gaol gang; Ann Bass, crown servant, is convicted of attempting to leave her place of employment, and sentenced to be put in stocks with an iron collar for two periods of eight hours, and to three months gaol.

Less obvious, but there in the background, is the unfolding tragedy of racial conflict:

> On Monday last while two men and two women were traveling with a cart and two bullocks on the Port Dalyrmple Road ... they were attacked by upwards of 50 Natives ... James Daley, one of the party, was obliged to fire with a pistol.
> *Hobart Town Gazette*, 19 October 1816

> When near shore the first object which attracted their sight was the corpse of their unfortunate companion [John Kemp, a sealer] lying at the water's edge, cut and mangled in a manner too shocking to relate ... the natives, who were in ambuscade [ambush], suddenly appeared on the beach armed with spears.
> *Hobart Town Gazette*, 28 November 1818

> On Tuesday last 300 sheep belonging to Mr James Triffitt ... were found dead ... the natives committed this great slaughter ... many [sheep] were much disfigured by having some of their eyes taken out and others with their backs broken.
> *Hobart Town Gazette*, 18 December 1819

The news reports never give a motive for the hostility, though one can guess that Kemp's shocking mutilation was castration, which gives a clue. But there was more to Aboriginal aggression than inexplicable malice, and the government knew it.

In May 1817, Lieutenant Governor William Sorell made an official proclamation: 'several Settlers and others are in the habit of maliciously and wantonly firing at, and destroying, the defenseless NATIVES or ABORIGINES of this island'. Sorell reiterated that the Aboriginals were under his protection, and that it was 'no less His ... Duty than it is his disposition to forbid and prevent, and when perpetrated to punish, any ill-treatment of the Native People of this Island'. He vowed to prosecute anyone committing 'any Act of Outrage or Aggression on the Native People'.

In 1819 Sorell again denounced 'Outrages ... recently perpetrated against some of the Native People', included the kidnapping of children. He said he was 'aware that many of the Settlers and Stock-keepers consider the Natives as a Hostile People, seeking without Provocation, Opportunities to destroy them and their Stock'. He believed this was untrue, stating that the native people

> are seldom the Assailants and that when they are, they act under the Impression of recent Injuries done to some of them by White People. It is undeniable that in many former instances Cruelties have been perpetrated repugnant to humanity and disgraceful to the British Character.

Settlers 'wantonly fire at and kill the Men ... pursue the Women' and kidnap children. 'This last Outrage is perhaps the most certain to excite in the sufferers a thirst for revenge, and to incite the Natives to take Vengeance indiscriminately.'

There is a terrifying impotence to these notices. In the beautiful landscape, a bloody tragedy was unfolding. Sorell knew it, but while he theoretically had the powers of a despot over the colony, in reality he could do little to stop it.

> **Settlers 'wantonly fire at and kill the Men ... pursue the Women' and kidnap children.**

THE BLACK WAR

When the first group of convicts and their military guardians arrived on the Derwent River in the autumn of 1804, the Aboriginal people could not have known that this marked the end of their world.

Europeans had visited before in ships, relations had generally been friendly, and the strangers had soon left. But this time the white men stayed, and although they nearly starved more than once, they established the town of Hobart. The economy of the penal colony was based on convict labour—not quite slavery, but with some of the attributes of a slave economy. It was a brutal and brutalising society.

As more free settlers arrived, and the areas taken over for farming and grazing expanded, a cycle of violence and retribution built up deadly momentum. The warning of Sorell's 1819 proclamation, that abuse would provoke vengeance, was realised. The 1820s saw vicious conflict: settlers were horribly murdered, farms burnt down, stock slaughtered. In response, the attitudes of most whites hardened further. They attacked the government for failing to protect them.

In 1828, a former editor of the *Hobart Town Gazette*, Andrew Bent, accused the lieutenant governor, now George Arthur, of 'a false notion of pity and humanity—a singular tenderness of consciousness [which] seems to keep the Executive from those positive and decided measures which can at once end all this dreadful carnage, and general terror'.

There was no doubt about what these 'positive' measures were: 'They are too ignorant—too truly barbarous to understand anything but *force* ... The Natives are never, in our opinion, to be quieted, otherwise than by one of two methods, viz. their extermination or their removal'.

Arthur had arrived in 1824. Like his predecessors, he believed that Aboriginal hostility was the result of past abuses by settlers. But the fighting had passed the point of no return. Arthur struggled to reconcile his Christian humanitarianism with the political realities of bloody and merciless conflict.

Periodically, the government did try to hold settlers to account for violence. In 1829, after one particularly horrible incident, the killing of a wounded Aboriginal woman at Emu Bay by a teenage convict servant, the government attempted to prosecute. Arthur's official papers record the argument and exchange of legal opinions about whether the killing was unlawful and, if so, who was culpable. The technical legalism may seem abstruse, and the result—no-one was punished—was palpably unjust. But the government took the case seriously and tried to enforce the law.

However, that law—which in effect permitted murder—was the government's own creation. In April 1828, Arthur declared martial law, banning Aboriginals from 'settled districts', where they could be shot on sight. In November, 'roving parties' were authorised to capture Aboriginals, with a reward of £5 for each adult and £2 for a child. Many of the roving parties simply killed their quarry. The Emu Bay killing was unusual only in that a serious effort was made to punish the perpetrator.

The Black War, as it became known, reached its climax in 1830, when almost the entire male settler population was mobilised to drive the remaining Aboriginals onto the Forestier Peninsula. This operation was an expensive failure—only two Aboriginals were captured—but it marked the end of serious conflict. By this time, the Aboriginals were so reduced in number and low in spirit that they were ready to surrender.

Arthur commissioned the remarkable George Augustus Robinson, a Methodist lay preacher from London, to travel into remote areas and persuade the Aboriginals to submit, promising them protection in return. Robinson was helped in what was called 'The Friendly Mission' by a native woman, Truganini, who saved his life more than once. Robinson was brave and dedicated and succeeded in his mission, but he was to prove a deadly friend. The surviving Aboriginals were gathered on Flinders Island, but it was a bleak and unsuitable location. Robinson, a sincere Christian, tried to convert the people, and encouraged a European diet and way of life. In an already traumatised community, the loss of culture broke the will of many. The mortality rate was appalling. Of the 201 Aboriginals who came to Flinders Island, only eighty-two were still alive when Robinson left them in 1838. In 1847, when the Aboriginals were allowed to move to a more suitable reserve on the mainland of Tasmania, there were only forty-seven left. The last survivor of this group was Truganini. She died in 1876.

Other Aboriginals had survived on islands in Bass Strait, and also on the mainland. The 1944 Census listed two 'full blood' as well as 377 'half-caste' Aboriginals in Tasmania. The premise of complete extinction, that Truganini was 'the last Tasmanian Aboriginal', was used against the surviving Indigenous community, but it was false.

Even so, Truganini's death was symbolic of an undeniable crime. The fate of the Tasmanians was a source of great embarrassment to the British Empire. It was, as Sorell said, 'repugnant to humanity and disgraceful to the British Character'. It called into question the moral basis of the Empire, and in turn the white settlement of Australia.

Like many emotive words, 'genocide' is sometimes used loosely. People wishing to preserve a minority language, for example, will talk of the failure to teach it in primary schools as 'cultural genocide'. At the other extreme, because genocide has a strict meaning in international law, hair-splitting legalism is sometimes used to defend the indefensible.

Under the relevant United Nations convention, genocide is defined as 'any of the following acts committed with intent to destroy, in whole or in part, a national, ethnical, racial or religious group'. These acts include killing members of the group, causing them serious bodily or mental harm, 'deliberately inflicting on the group conditions of life calculated to bring about its physical destruction in whole or in part', imposing 'measures intended to prevent births' within the group, and forcibly transferring children to another group.

In the case of the Tasmanian Aboriginals, it can be argued that the authorities *did not intend* to wipe them out. Indeed, they tried, though ineffectually, to protect them—the killings were mostly unofficial and illegal. But government policy by 1830—forced removal under the threat of death—was genocidal. Ultimately so was Robinson's mission. Though he meant to rescue the Aboriginals, he was party to their removal from the land and the destruction of their traditional culture, something which proved as deadly as bullets.

Genocide is a modern word, coined in 1944. The UN convention that defined it as a crime was drafted in 1948. It is right to be cautious when applying moral and legal concepts retrospectively. But the abuse and murder of the Aboriginals was wrong by the moral and legal standards of the time, and there were those who condemned it as such. A religiously minded correspondent wrote to the *Hobart Town Gazette* in 1818:

> Were the Almighty, by an audible voice from Heaven, to call upon every one, abetting or visiting those scenes of cruelty, saying 'Where is thy brother? The voice of thy brother's blood crieth unto me from the ground'. What could he answer?

> Say not there is no relation between us; for has not the Creator 'made of one blood, all nations of men, for to dwell on all the face of the earth'?

What happened in Tasmania was the deliberate and systematic destruction of a people.

MEMORY AND DENIAL

Because Tasmania is an island, and because its people were racially distinct, the genocide that took place there was beyond denial. However, on the mainland all 'Australian Aboriginals' could be grouped together, and the destruction of a particular tribe could be masked somewhat. But the story was very often the same.

When the Victorian Western District was settled in the 1840s, many of those taking up new sheep runs had come from Van Diemen's Land and were veterans of the Black War. The killing continued.

In one instance of many, Aboriginals stole about fifty sheep from two brothers named Whyte, who had a run near the Wando River north of Portland. A neighbour, JG Robertson, described what happened when the shepherds caught up with the Aboriginals:

> They had taken shelter in an open plain with a long clump of tea-tree, which the Whyte Brothers' party, seven in number, surrounded and shot them all but one. Fifty-one men were killed, and the bones of the men and sheep lay together, bleaching in the sun.

The violence of the pastoral frontier was not universal, but it was without question widespread. Sometimes it was avowedly genocidal. Ernestine Hill, in her history of the Northern Territory, recounts an incident in which a man justifies the murder of Aboriginal children: 'Nits is lice'.

Those who survived faced what historian Robert Kenny calls the ruptured world. The previous ways of understanding the world and living in it were no longer viable: how to adjust, how to live, when so much had been lost, when so much had changed?

The Tasmanian Aboriginal genocide, along with the many other local, less-famous conflicts that resulted in 'extermination or removal', was also a disaster for white Australia. The dark and bloody story created guilt and a bad conscience which is still with us. This guilt manifests in two main ways. One is a defensive racism, demonising and ridiculing Aboriginals for faults real and imagined. The other is the romanticising of all things Aboriginal, an overcompensation which makes any criticism of any Aboriginal person or group impossible.

Both manifestations are damaging. Political correctness has at times allowed abuses in Aboriginal organisations and communities to go unexposed and unchecked. Among historians it has led to a certain sloppiness, a slide into careless overstatement. This has been particularly harmful in allowing a denialist attack on the whole body of Aboriginal history. Keith Windschuttle, in his book *The Fabrication of Aboriginal History*, argued that various historians—he calls

The violence of the pastoral frontier was not universal, but it was without question widespread.

them 'orthodox'—were driven by ideology to create a false 'genocidal' history. He accused the orthodox of 'abandoning truth and objectivity', the result being 'the politicization of history'.

The notion that stories of massacre and genocide are a recent invention of politically correct historians is unjustifiable. RH Milford, the grumpy ex-soldier who travelled around Australia in 1932, recounted several stories of murder and abuse. Ernestine Hill wrote her history of the Northern Territory in the late 1940s; mass killings of Aboriginals, then in living memory, were common knowledge.

> **Simple acknowledgment of the truth was uncontroversial in Australia until well after World War II.**

Edward Shann, an economist and historian whose enthusiasm for free markets made him a conservative icon, wrote an economic history of Australia that was published in 1930. Shann is blunt in his assessment of the place of the murder and exploitation of Aboriginals in the economy of settler pastoralism: 'No disagreement between the whites ... prevented their joining to treat the myalls ["untamed" Aboriginals] as vermin whose destruction was to be achieved by any means, from shot-guns to poisoned damper'.

Such a simple acknowledgment of the truth was uncontroversial in Australia until well after World War II. The 1949 *Australian Yearbook*, for example, matter-of-factly notes the killing and abuse of Aboriginals, especially by pastoralists, as background to the condition and numbers of Australian Aboriginals at that time. It was only with increased

Aboriginal activism from the 1960s onwards, especially the land rights movement, that Aboriginal history developed economic and political implications. What Edward Shann had plainly acknowledged suddenly threatened the legal and moral basis for the ownership of cattle runs and mineral resources. It was the denial of Aboriginal genocide—a deliberate forgetting—not the history of that genocide, that was the modern invention.

Windschuttle did identify some errors in the use of evidence by some historians, but by no measure did he sustain his case that the Tasmanian Aboriginal genocide was a tissue of lies. However, the very existence of a thick book called *The Fabrication of Aboriginal History* made denial possible.

In 2004, Prime Minister John Howard told the media he was reading the book and regarded it as a contribution to reversing 'the tide of political correctness'. Howard said: 'Australia is more self-confident, it doesn't feel the need to explain itself, we don't have perpetual self-identity seminars any more'. But true self-confidence, of nations as of people, must be based on self-knowledge. This means acknowledging the past, including the unpleasant bits. As long as the disaster of genocide is not fully acknowledged, the disaster of denial continues.

JG Robertson, the settler whose account of a massacre of Aboriginals near the Wando River was cited above, wrote a long letter to the lieutenant governor of Victoria, Charles Joseph La Trobe, telling of his experiences. In addition to the Wando incident, he described in detail several murders of Aboriginals of which he had personal knowledge, and many others which were common knowledge.

> I have on four different occasions, when they [Aboriginals] committed murders, gone out with others in search of them, and *I now thank my God* I never fell in with them, or there is no doubt I should be like many others and feel that sting that must always be felt by the most regardless of the deed done to those poor creatures ... [original emphasis]
>
> I will here change the subject, for it is too painful to dwell on ...

For many years, Australia found the uglier truths of its past too painful to dwell on, and, like JG Robertson, changed the subject.

The spread of rabbits across Australia was the most rapid animal colonisation in world history.
(National Archives of Australia: A1200, L44186)

5

FERAL NATION: RABBITS, 1859 TO THE PRESENT

Australia has a host of introduced pests: feral pigs, feral horses, feral cats, foxes, starlings, sparrows, pigeons, Indian mynas, European carp, prickly pear, lantana, water hyacinth, and literally hundreds of others. Cane toads are probably the most famous. But nothing can compare in its devastating impact on the Australian environment to the European rabbit. It is one of the great environmental catastrophes, not just in our own history, but on a world scale.

In Richard Adams' novel *Watership Down*, a group of rabbits flee their home warren, which is faced with destruction. The leader of the runaways, Hazel, imagines the place they need to find: 'I know what we ought to be looking for. A high, lonely place with dry soil, where we can see and hear all around, and men hardly ever come'. And after much danger and adventure, they find their haven—quite a feat, as the story is set in England—Watership Down.

Adams' novel is a fantasy, but it does contain some truth. He describes how rabbits are conservative animals, set in their ways. Their social structures are ruthless, enforced with violence. When rabbits come to maturity, they are usually forced to leave the warren—they will often loiter near the closest neighbour until they are either accepted or killed. Only catastrophe—the destruction of the warren, starvation—will cause rabbits to move in large numbers. And once they find a new place to live, they establish the same social order as before.

Adams' description of a promised land for rabbits is accurate too. With its vast stretches of thinly populated dry grasslands, Australia is one vast Watership Down.

The European rabbit, *Oryctologus cuniculus*, is one of those species which has thrived in company with humans. Its major spread as a wild animal has only occurred in recent historical times, usually with human assistance. As European ships developed their global trading routes, rabbits were often released onto islands to provide food for sailors. They are now present on some 800 islands around the world, as well as in parts of the Americas. But it is in Australia that rabbits have thrived best.

When rabbits first began colonising Australia, it was free from many old world diseases, and they were faced with few natural predators. Rabbits were able to take over existing warrens dug by native animals such as wombats and bilbies. The new conditions created by European graziers suited rabbits too: lots of cut timber for cover, and grazed pastures with nutritious regrowth.

The first known 'successful' release of rabbits in Australia occurred near the Victorian town of Geelong in 1859. By 1890 they had reached southern Queensland, and a decade later had arrived in the Northern Territory and Western Australia.

By 1980 they were firmly established across the continent in latitudes south of the Tropic of Capricorn, although even north of the tropic there are small colonies.

It is an animal colonisation without equal in natural history. In little more than a century, the European rabbit had become one of the most widely distributed mammals in Australia. Except for the house mouse, it is also the most abundant. The rate of spread averaged between 10 and 15 kilometres per year but at times was much faster—in marginal areas, up to 100 kilometres per year. It was, a 1995 Commonwealth Scientific and Industrial Research Organisation (CSIRO) report notes, 'the fastest rate of any colonising mammal anywhere in the world'.

And when the rabbits arrived, they were like a swarm of locusts. They would eat all the grass, and then the bark off bushes and trees. Thousands of sheep starved to death. If wheat had been planted, the rabbits ate that too. In some semi-arid areas the rabbits killed every shrub and tree, reducing hundreds of square kilometres to desert. In some places they would run up against a rabbit-proof fence and die at the base. The dead would pile up in the corners until eventually the living would scramble over them, spilling over the fence.

One South Australian farmer wrote:

> No-one would believe the mischief the rabbits are doing unless they could see it ... many of the runs are so bare there is not

grass enough to feed the rabbits, let alone the sheep ... the rabbits are travelling in thousands in search of food.

He described one of these mass migrations: 'I met a swarm coming from the hills. I never saw such a thing before. The ground was scarcely to be seen for a mile in length'. Within five weeks of the first arrival of rabbits, he added, 'we have killed thousands. When the sun is hot you can go along the fences or any place where it is shady and kill hundreds with a stick ... The paddocks stink with the dead ones'.

The key to the success of the European rabbit is the warren. Rabbits can live above ground—and often do where there is sufficient cover—but the warren allows them to thrive in open grasslands. Because they live in large social groups, they can create extensive warrens, deep and complex enough to provide protection from predators and shelter from the weather. Some are vast, and if mapped would resemble the London Underground—one warren is recorded as having 150 entrances and a total tunnel length of more than 500 metres. More common are warrens with three to fifteen entrances.

Rabbits can expand their numbers very quickly when conditions are favourable, especially if there are empty warrens to move into. A female rabbit is sexually mature at three months of age. The gestation period is only thirty days, and litters are large: usually there are between four and seven young. The mother can successfully mate again within hours of giving birth; a typical female rabbit will have between ten and fifteen young in one year.

This is one reason why the rabbit is such a curse to Australian farmers. Our climate is inconsistent, with periods of good rain and drought seasons. Rabbits breed explosively in good seasons. The population crashes in drought, but not before it destroys the pasture it shares with stock animals, badly degrading the land. The teeth and claws of rabbits will not just crop the grass but dig up the roots. They will also ringbark trees, stripping the land bare. And when rains come again, the surviving rabbits can quickly replace their numbers, recolonising abandoned warrens.

The rabbit is without question the most serious pest in Australia. In narrow economic terms alone the cost of rabbits runs to hundreds of millions of dollars per year. By competing with livestock for feed, they reduce the carrying capacity of farms—twelve to sixteen rabbits eat the same amount of pasture as one sheep.

More serious in the long term is the environmental damage rabbits do.

More serious in the long term is the environmental damage rabbits do. They cause erosion and compete with native animals for food and habitat—in some cases pushing species such as the bilby to the point of extinction. Many native tree species, especially in semi-arid regions, face annihilation: mature trees are not damaged, but the rabbits eat every seedling before it has a chance to grow. In many areas, stands of mulga and she-oak are doomed. Even one rabbit per hectare is enough to prevent regeneration, and so when the mature trees die they will not be replaced.

TWELVE BREEDING PAIRS AND ONE IDIOT

The story of how rabbits came to be such a problem in Australia is usually told something like this. It all began in 1859 when Thomas Austin, an English farmer with aristocratic pretensions, imported twelve breeding pairs from England and let them go at his property, Barwon Downs, near Geelong. It is a comforting tale. It was the fault of one idiot, who let the genie out of the bottle.

But the truth is much more complicated. Thomas Austin did bring in rabbits and let them run free. Within a few years he had thousands of them, and he was proud of it, hosting shooting parties and giving breeding pairs away. But lots of other people had tried to establish rabbits in Australia. There were five rabbits on the First Fleet, another consignment to New South Wales in 1791, another in 1806. In the 1820s, rabbits were successfully introduced to Tasmania. When Victoria and South Australia were settled from the 1830s, many people farmed rabbits, and they were running wild near Port Lincoln. The HMS *Beagle*, on her famous voyage of discovery, encountered rabbits on several Australian islands in 1842, and her commander carried several pairs aboard, letting them off on islands likely to prove hospitable. The police station established at Port Phillip had a rabbit warren underneath it in the 1840s. Concerted efforts were made to establish rabbits in the wild near Castlemaine, in Victoria, in the same period.

Put simply, the European settlers of Australia *worked hard* to introduce rabbits. They were a luxury food and a rabbit warren was a status possession, the mark of a landed gentleman. Thomas Austin is famous for it, but there were plenty of others who had tried. Some releases, including at least one in South Australia, had already been successful. And if Austin's twenty-four animals had all been eaten by a dingo after they were released, lots of other people would have continued the effort. We were, as a society, determined to have rabbits, and we eventually got our wish.

The response to rabbits in Australia has often been as stupid as the decision to introduce them. One solution that was tried—despite many warnings that it would do more harm than good—was the release of large numbers of domestic cats into the wild, in the hope they would keep the rabbits down. The cats had little impact on the rabbits: they killed plenty, but nothing the rabbits could not replace, and they ate a lot of other animals, becoming a serious pest in their own right.

But perhaps the greatest foolishness was the erection, at great public expense, of vast 'rabbit-proof' fences, designed to keep parts of Australia rabbit-free. The first was built in the 1880s to protect northern New South Wales—it eventually ran some 1100 kilometres. Others were built in Queensland and, most famously, in Western Australia, where Rabbit-proof Fence No. 1, said to be the longest unbroken fence in the world, stretched for 1833 kilometres from near Esperance to the coast between Broome and Port Headland. Fence No. 1 had to be linked up to fences No. 2 and No. 3, because by the time No. 1 was finished, the rabbits were already past it.

The expense of building these fences was colossal: £400 000 for the West Australian barrier alone. It is a peculiar reflection on the way our society works that it can take a long time for a government to commit to an expensive project like the rabbit-proof fence, but that once begun, nothing—not even obvious rabbit infestations on the other side—will stop it.

Admittedly, much of the fence building took place during a recession, and the fences did at least provide employment. But that was the only real benefit. As a rabbit-control measure, the fences were a complete waste of time. They could be damaged by kangaroos, wombats or other large animals, or by flooding, fire or severe storms. Sometimes erosion would open gaps beneath the fences. Sometimes sand or debris would build up against them, allowing rabbits to walk over the top. There had to be gates for people to get through, and these were not always closed. And sometimes people carried a sack of rabbits across the fence, not caring about the consequences.

Eloquent testimony to the uselessness of the rabbit-proof fence can be found in a celebratory history of Western Australia published in the 1950s. 'Though the fences were repaired and patrolled, they did not achieve their original purpose ... In later years they proved useful in keeping out marauding dingos and emus.' It is hard to imagine a marauding emu being much deterred by a fence standing 3 feet, 7 inches (109 centimetres) high. In any event, as emus and dingos have existed across the whole of Western Australia for millennia, which side of the fence were they being kept 'out' of?

Various ways of poisoning rabbits were tried, too. But again, great effort and expense were incurred for little result. Trapping and shooting did little but keep the rabbit population healthy by thinning out the weaker and slower animals.

> **For many years, the voices of those who made their livelihoods from rabbits were loud and influential.**

The farmer, poet and historian Eric Rolls memorably described the Australian preference for effort over planning:

> One fault of the Australian man-on-the-land is his penchant for hard work. He believes that it is disgraceful to sit down and think. If he is not losing sweat he is not working. If he were found reading a book on soil conservation at 10 am, he would feel ashamed. But if someone found him ringbarking the last four trees in one of his cultivation paddocks and called him hard-working, he would feel proud.

Rolls is wrong to regard this attitude as a rural vice: it is a rare Australian organisation—whether a small business, large company, public sector agency or government department—that does not overvalue visible busyness. If the activity generates money, no matter what hidden losses and long-term damage might be involved, so much the better.

For many years, the voices of those who made their livelihoods from rabbits were loud and influential. The Commonwealth Government even had a statutory agency, the Rabbit Skins Board, to regulate prices and protect the interests of the hard-working rabbiters. Rabbit fur was used to make hats—including the Australian Army slouch hat—and so the industry did well during wartime. In the late 1940s, rabbits were at their peak in Australia. In 1948, 130 million rabbits were caught and killed—the total population was unknown, but must have been many times this figure. The rabbit industry was worth perhaps £4 million pounds per year. But the annual cost of damage to pastures and crops was estimated at £12 million—and that was a figure which took no account of destruction to non-agricultural land.

Any suggestion of serious measures to reduce rabbit numbers was bitterly opposed by the rabbiters. They were especially opposed to the use of the disease myxomatosis.

+ + +

Myxomatosis is a horrible disease. Its name is derived from the Greek word for 'slime'. Once a rabbit is infected with the myxoma virus—perhaps by being bitten by a flea or mosquito which has recently fed on an infected animal—after about a week of incubation, its eyes begin to shed a watery discharge. This thickens, and the eyelids also swell, blinding the animal behind lesions encrusted with hardened yellow matter. The genitals, nose and ears erupt in the same way, and jelly-like bulges appear on other parts of the body. Death results as quickly as thirteen days after infection, but can take longer.

The myxoma virus was identified in 1898 when it swept through the stock of laboratory rabbits at a research institute in Montevideo, Uruguay, killing almost all of them. The virus is present in native American species of rabbit but is benign to them: it is, however, lethal to the European rabbit. Australian scientists became aware of the disease and its potential in 1919, but there was little enthusiasm for further research. Scientists were worried about damaging the rabbit trade, and in any case, 'popular sentiment here is opposed to the extermination of the rabbit by the use of some virulent organism'. There were some experiments in the 1920s, but the results were unpromising.

Then in 1933 Dr Jean Macnamara, a Melbourne paediatrician, visited New York to further her expertise in the treatment of polio. There she met another researcher, Dr Richard Shope, an expert on animal viruses. Shope was researching myxomatosis because in Canada it was a threat to rabbit farming. Macnamara was able to persuade the Australian Government to support more research in London, and in 1936 the Council for Scientific and Industrial Research (later the CSIRO) began tests in Australia. These tests were not successful, partly because the rabbit industry furiously opposed field tests, and because the only site available was in a dry part of South Australia—myxomatosis is usually spread by insects, such as mosquitoes, and these are more common in wet areas. The disease did not spread, the researchers concluded that it had little value, and the project was wound up in 1943.

But in 1949, the redoubtable Macnamara—Dame Jean, since 1935, for her work on polio—rejoined the fray. Macnamara wrote to newspapers and lobbied politicians and farmers' groups and anyone else who would listen, spreading her message that myxomatosis should be persisted with. In 1950, the Victorian Government finally supported another trial, and the CSIRO cooperated. The first release was unsuccessful; a CSIRO press release stated: 'Myxo fails against rabbits'.

A second, near Albury, produced no result for some time, but then sick rabbits began to appear, in greater and greater numbers.

The plague spread into Victoria and the New South Wales Riverina, leaving a stinking blanket of dead rabbits, the survivors stumbling blind into dams and creeks and drowning, fouling the water. Some people were worried that the disease might affect other animals or even humans—an outbreak of human encephalitis in Mildura and Shepparton caused some alarm until myxomatosis was ruled out as a cause—but only rabbits were affected. Within nine weeks of the first signs of the disease, an area of nearly 2 million square kilometres was infected; by 1954 the disease had spread across the entire continent. In many instances, the mortality rate may have been as high as 99 per cent.

There were those who were horrified by myxomatosis. Rabbiters made threatening phone calls to Jean Macnamara. Others were distressed by the sheer suffering caused. In England, the Royal Society for the Prevention of Cruelty to Animals (RSPCA) ran strong campaigns against the introduction of the disease there in the 1950s. The RSPCA argued that the disease 'kills only after intense, prolonged pain and misery' and that 'rabbit control can be maintained by humane methods'. There may have been truth to this view in England, but in Australia the case was different. 'Humane' methods had no hope of controlling rabbits here. The pattern of explosive breeding meant that millions of the animals would, periodically, suffer horrible deaths from starvation and thirst, and in the meantime destroy vegetation and cause the starvation of livestock and native animals.

Myxomatosis was, and still is, undeniably cruel. But in the 1950s, for Australia's farmers and those who cared about the Australian environment, the disease had the quality of divine intervention.

Jean Macnamara had some fine qualities: toughness, energy and a dedication to her cause. But her triumph was achieved by a troubling process, one too common in Australia and which, as a people still learning how to live in a fragile land, we can ill-afford. Problems of environment and land management are complex. The best chance of good answers lies in careful observation, detailed research and analysis—and in the exchange of information and ideas through open and constructive debate. But Macnamara was autocratic, impatient of those she regarded as fools. She publicly attacked scientists who had come to different conclusions, deriding their 'pathetically limited inquiry'. She relentlessly criticised the CSIRO. Fixated on myxomatosis, she personalised the scientific argument and needlessly antagonised her colleagues.

Macnamara was vindicated by the results: she was right about myxomatosis. But the astonishing spread of the disease—like the spread of rabbits themselves, almost without parallel—was a matter of luck as much as science. More often then not, turning scientific inquiry into personalised politics will produce poor results.

Myxomatosis was unfortunate in another respect. It killed astonishing numbers of rabbits, but some survived. Those survivors acquired some immunity, and with their extraordinary capacity to breed, subsequent generations have steadily recolonised their old haunts. Rabbits have shown time and again their astonishing ability to rebound. In one controlled study, myxomatosis reduced a population of 260 rabbits to two—a male and a female. Within eighteen months the population had recovered to 184, before another outbreak of the disease again reduced the population.

The suddenness and apparent completeness with which myxomatosis swept rabbits away also caused complacency among landowners. Scientists lament the 'myth of the super bug', blind faith in the idea that some new biological control agent will turn up and, like myxomatosis, wipe the pests away. Meanwhile, landowners neglect more-traditional methods of control.

In the mid 1990s a new virus, rabbit haemorrhagic disease (RHD), was being considered as a control measure. After extensive reviews of what was known of the disease, a research program began, along with an extensive process of consultation and an attempt to assess its costs, benefits and risks. All this became redundant, however, when in 1995 RHD appeared in rabbits in South Australia, not far from where it was being trialled on Wardang Island. Its hand forced, the CSIRO proceeded to release the disease more widely.

As with myxomatosis, we were lucky. The disease has been effective in reducing rabbit numbers, especially in the semi-arid regions where they do the most damage. Even luckier,

RHD has not affected other animals—native or livestock. Within a few years, RHD was being reported as a success story, a sign of hope.

But the RHD episode is troubling. The disease was released into the wild either deliberately or by accident, and it is hard to know which is worse. Either someone continued in the steps of Thomas Austin, recklessly unleashing a potent new life form into the Australian environment, or Australia's peak research body was unable to guarantee the security of biological trials.

THE GREY BLANKET

Such was the early success of RDH in significantly reducing rabbit numbers that, in 2003, one environmental magazine ran the headline: 'Australia after rabbits'. In many semi-arid areas, native tree seedlings were appearing—and surviving—for the first time in decades. The predator populations that fed on rabbits—especially foxes and feral cats—had also declined, giving hope that native species might recover. But the article ended on a low note: 'Caution is advisable because we know from the myxomatosis experience that RHD may give us just a 10–15-year window of opportunity before rabbits again bounce back'.

So it is proving.

Some friends recently invited my family to stay with them in rural Victoria. The trip was like a time warp: *the rabbits!* Not just one or two at dusk, but dozens and dozens of them in broad daylight, along the verge of the roads, in open paddocks, sheltering under windbreaks. Our children were excited and thought the animals were cute—which, from a distance, they are.

I felt an eerie recognition. I knew rabbits like this only from history. This was a hint of the 'grey blanket' the colonial settlers described in their letters. RH Milford, on his journey around Australia in 1932, mentions casually, as an aside, 'running down hundreds of rabbits that dashed into the glare of the headlights' during a night drive on the Nullarbor.

The scene I witnessed in central Victoria was a glimpse of the past—and perhaps of the future, too. Rabbits in plague numbers. A devastated agriculture. Humans retreating from the land, abandoning it to rabbits and the desert. It has happened before.

Watching the approach of the fire front, 13 January 1939. The Black Friday bushfires burned 10 percent of the land surface of Victoria. (Department of Primary Industries, Victoria)

6
BLACK FRIDAY, 1939 AND BEYOND

Drop a match into a field of dry grass on a still day and the fire will burn outwards, forming a steadily expanding circle. If the fire is on a slope, the flames heading uphill will reach fresh fuel more easily and spread more quickly, turning the circle into an ellipse. A breeze will have the same effect. A strong wind may drive the back edge of the fire perimeter in on itself, snuffing it out altogether, while the forward edge will form a horseshoe shape: the centre, where burning is strongest, is the head of the fire. Weaker fire burns along the flanks.

These simple patterns are made much more complex by rough country and by forests, but generally a relatively cool fire burning on the forest floor will behave predictably. But when fire climbs, its nature changes and it becomes far more dangerous. And the Australian forest has evolved to help fire climb.

Eucalyptus trees dominate the vegetation of Australia to an extent unmatched by any genus of plant on any other continent. The two secrets to their success are the ability to survive in a dry and erratic climate, and to thrive in combination with fire. Other sorts of forest, especially the pines and firs of Siberia and North America, are affected by fire.

Other dry lands have plants which need fire to regenerate, like the proteas of southern Africa. But nowhere else in the world has the forest evolved to burn so readily, and with such fury.

The eucalyptus tree is a 'fire weed'. Some survive fires that would kill most other species. Others, like the majestic mountain ash, *only* reproduce in the wake of a calamitous fire. The mature trees are killed, but their hard woody seeds rain down and germinate in the ashes. The trees of the new forest rise together, like a field of wheat—they have little competition, because every other seed has been killed.

Because it survives fire so much better than its ecological competitors, the eucalyptus has evolved to encourage fire. Eucalyptus leaves are full of flammable oil. The bark peels off in long strips which hang in ropes to the forest floor. In the right conditions, an existing fire which appears under control can climb these ropes into the treetops. There the wind is stronger, carrying fire from tree to tree. 'Crowning' is fast, unpredictable, deadly. Burning embers are thrown far ahead, starting new fires. Given a dry forest, low humidity and a hot wind, the blaze can build into a cyclone of flame, the most terrifying of natural disasters.

Little is known about the patterns of Aboriginal burning in most areas, but it is beyond doubt that fire was used extensively and deliberately. Periodic patchwork burning of

> 'Crowning' is fast, unpredictable, deadly. Burning embers are thrown far ahead, starting new fires. Given a dry forest, low humidity and a hot wind, the blaze can build into a cyclone of flame, the most terrifying of natural disasters.

the country promoted the growth of new grass and kept the understorey of forests clear of scrub, reducing the frequency of calamitous fire. These systems of firestick farming, honed for thousands of years, were abruptly swept aside by white settlement. The newcomers burnt too, but their fires were uncoordinated, their actions uninformed. Fuel loads built up in the forests, and flammable scrub flourished in what had been grasslands.

+ + +

In 1851, a dry summer culminated in a day with high temperatures, a hot northerly wind and low humidity. On 6 February, which became known as Black Thursday, the settlement of Port Phillip—soon to become the colony of Victoria—burned. From Gippsland to the Western District, fires ripped across grassland and through scrub and forest. The sky was darkened as far away as Tasmania and the sun turned blood-red. Farms were destroyed, thousands of animals were killed, and ten people were known to have died: almost certainly there were other casualties in remote areas.

For most settlers a fire driven by a hot gale, tearing through a forest which did not just burn but exploded, was something completely outside their experience. The shock and fear of the day inspired a visiting English artist, William Strutt, to paint his remarkable *Black Thursday, February 6th, 1851*. The huge canvas, 3 metres wide, now hangs in the State Library of Victoria. It shows people and animals fleeing in stark terror from the fires, and remains one of the very few works of art to capture the emotional experience of a bushfire—or to even tackle the subject.

Fire does not feature strongly in Australian art or popular culture which is surprising given that bushfire is a signature Australian experience. The Australian ecosystem is dominated by fire to an extent unmatched anywhere else in the world. But you would not guess it from our art. It is a strange and dangerous absence. We forget about fire.

After 1851, bushfire disasters became periodic, something that happened every twenty or twenty-five years. Some fires were bad enough to be given names. The first day of February 1898, for example, was called 'Red Tuesday'. This fire followed a heatwave which tormented the colonial statesmen gathered in Melbourne to thrash out the details of Federation. During the height of the fires, smoke drifted into Parliament House, where the convention was sitting. It seems appropriate that the Australian nation was shaped in this setting: the founding fathers in their three-piece woollen suits gasping for breath.

Serious bushfires occurred again in 1919, 1926 and 1932. The 1926 fires culminated in Black Sunday, 14 February. Thirty-one people were killed; fourteen, including a 3-month-old baby, died at Worlley's timber mill at Mt Beenak, east of Melbourne. It was typical of many small mill settlements scattered throughout the mountain ash forests of Victoria. Set deep in the forest, the mill could only be reached by a narrow-gauge tramway. The fire cut the tramway, and the people were trapped.

After six mill workers were killed in the 1932 fires, the Victorian Forests Commission began to urge mill owners to establish a safe refuge for their workers, in the form of a dugout. This was to be built in a cleared area and topped with a thick layer of earth. 'It is pointed out', said a commission letter in 1933, 'that on you does the preservation of the lives of your mill employees and their families largely depend, and unless suitable precautions are taken now it is quite possible that a disaster similar to those of 1926 and 1932 may occur'. Some mill owners were spurred into action, while others made various excuses or just refused to act.

There was an unusual spike in global temperatures in the late 1930s, which peaked in 1938 and 1939 and led to one of the first predictions of global warming. In Australia it caused a severe drought. Rainfall was well below average across south-eastern Australia, and as the hot, dry weather continued it was clear that the summer of 1938–39 would be a bad fire season.

The reality, however, outstripped anyone's worst fears.

BLACK FRIDAY

As early as August 1938—still technically winter in southern Australia—serious fires broke out across Victoria. Some were caused by lightning, others by graziers burning off, still others by carelessly lit campfires. More than 200 fires were burning as 1938 came to an end.

Early in the new year, the weather turned hotter, and strong winds began to blow from the north. By Sunday 8 January, the fires were becoming serious: more than 100 houses were destroyed that day, along with several timber mills. On Tuesday 10 January, the wind strengthened again and the fires expanded. People were killed, including a family who tried to escape fire by car and were trapped when a tree fell across the road. Several more timber mills were destroyed.

The men, women and children of the little mill settlements sheltered in dugouts—where dugouts had been built. There, people were reasonably safe, but surviving the fires meant a long struggle with heat, the threat of suffocation, and terror.

The next two days provided some respite: it was cooler, and the wind had dropped. But vast fires still burned, and on Friday 13 January, the worst fire weather yet experienced turned Victoria into an inferno.

The worst fire weather yet experienced turned Victoria into an inferno.

The famous writer HG Wells was in Melbourne on Black Friday. He got into trouble for describing Adolph Hitler as a 'certifiable lunatic'—in accordance with British policy, the Australian Government was anxious not to offend Germany—and said that the war he feared was coming might be like the bushfires. A better comparison would have been the war which Wells had imagined forty years earlier. In *The War of the Worlds*, invading Martians kill with two weapons: an intense heat ray and the Black Smoke, a poison gas which settles like soot over its victims. Bushfire kills in the same ways: with blasts of radiant heat or thick choking smoke.

The conditions experienced on Black Friday were such that nothing could be done to stop the fires. The temperature in Melbourne peaked at 45.6 degrees Celsius, a record not broken until 2009. The humidity was almost inconceivably low: 8 per cent. And howling from the north was a hot, gale-force wind.

The fires were whipped into tornadoes of flame so powerful that giant trees were snapped off halfway up their length, like broken matches. Driven by the wind, and creating their own violent updrafts, the fires raged beyond all hope of control. One fire in the north-east of the state, was estimated to have travelled more than 100 kilometres in one evening. Almost the entire Victorian Alps, from the Murray River to the La Trobe Valley, was burnt. Meanwhile, other fires burned in southern New South Wales, the Australian Capital Territory, western Victoria and South Australia—the ash from these fires fell as far away as New Zealand.

One man jumped into a water tank; the water heated and killed him. Others tried to run, but there was nowhere to run to.

Many of those who died on Black Friday were mill workers and their families, who were trapped deep in the burning forest. Some survived by sheltering in rivers and dams, or in dugouts. But in other places, where the warnings and advice of Forests Commission officers had been ignored year after year, there was no refuge.

Fitzpatrick's mill was located in a region of forest known as Matlock. Scrub grew thickly up to the edge of the settlement. When the fire came, the sixteen men there had little hope. Some burrowed into a large heap of sawdust, apparently thinking that it would protect them from the heat. But the sawdust burned and they died. One man jumped into a water tank; the water heated and killed him. Others tried to run, but there was nowhere to run to, and their bodies were found where the heat and smoke overcame them. The mill horses were trapped in their stalls and died there, struggling against their harnesses.

Only one man survived, wrapped in a wet blanket on a small patch of clear ground. Sparks set the blanket alight but he beat out the flames with his bare hands. Breathing through the blanket, he stayed still, resisting the urge to run, while around him the mill and the forest burned and his friends died.

A royal commissioner later wrote of this tragedy—the worst of many similar tragedies—that the 'full story of the killing of this small community is one of unpreparedness, because of apathy and ignorance and perhaps of something worse'.

By Friday night, the wind had dropped. Fires still burned: more towns were almost destroyed over the subsequent weekend. But the worst of the crisis was over and by Sunday rain was falling in the west of the state, reaching the east by the following day. The creeks and rivers ran black.

As remote communities were reached by relief workers, the staggering scale of the disaster became apparent. Ten per cent of the surface area of Victoria was burnt. Tens of thousands of animals had been killed; thousands more were so badly injured they had to be shot. The towns of Narbethong, Noojee, Nayook West, Hill End and Woods Point were destroyed, as were sixty-nine sawmills. About 1500 people had lost their homes. In total, seventy-one people died in Victoria, and six in other states. Hundreds of people had been badly injured, and thousands more were traumatised by their encounters with death or by the loss of loved ones.

This terrible human cost was hidden: few people spoke of the horrors they had witnessed. Forty years later, WS Noble, a journalist who had himself been trapped by fire while covering Black Friday, wrote:

> Only those who have heard the heart-chilling roar of the racing fires, with the booming of exploding clouds of gas, know what a test of nerves men and women—and children—passed through. It says something for the Australian character of that time that there were no reports of psychiatric cases in the wake of that week.

The incidence of suicide, alcoholism and similar problems among the survivors of Black Friday is not known, but if similar disasters are any guide, several thousand people must have been affected in such ways. Those who recovered would have been burdened by guilt and grief. Historian Peter Evans (no relation) interviewed many survivors of Black Friday: some, even half a century on, broke down in tears as they spoke of the disaster.

On one issue, though, denial was impossible. The magnitude of Black Friday forced the people of rural Australia to reassess their relationship with the land, with fire, and with each other. A key actor in this change was the man appointed to conduct the royal commission which investigated the fires: Leonard Stretton.

Stretton was a lawyer and dedicated social reformer who had risen from humble origins—his father was a brewery clerk—to be a judge at the age of just forty-three. Within weeks of rain dousing the last outbreak of fire, Stretton began touring the devastated countryside. The hot weather returned, but Stretton sat taking evidence from foresters and mill workers, farmers and firefighters, police and public servants. The hearings continued until April. The evidence ran to thousands of pages. Stretton wrote in his report: 'The truth was hard to find ... Much of the evidence was coloured by self-interest. Much of it was quite false. Little of it was wholly truthful'.

Stretton was a man of rare insight and moral sense. In his report, he cut through the blaming and denial to the core truth behind the disaster: society, all of us, was responsible.

There were immediate causes for particular fires, and he recommended changes to the law, to local government regulations and to the organisation of the Forests Commission to prevent these from recurring. The Black Friday fires were also unusually destructive because there had been a severe drought followed by severe weather. But beyond that, 'the causes of the 1939 bushfires were no different from those of any other summer':

> The major, over-riding cause, which comprises all others, is the indifference with which forest fires, as a menace to the interests of us all, have been regarded. They have

been considered to be matters of individual interest, for treatment by individuals.

People carelessly and selfishly lit fires; they carelessly and selfishly allowed them to burn. 'These fires', Stretton wrote, in a phrase which would become famous, 'were lit by the hand of man'.

One of the great foundation myths of Australian history is that of settler solidarity, that the pioneers confronting a harsh environment helped each other in adversity. Such mutual help, given without hesitation or request, did occur. In *On the Wool Track*, CEW Bean tells of how dozens of men working on an outback station spent exhausting days and nights fighting a scrub fire that threatened a neighbour's property. Bean later remarked that this courage and selflessness was a prelude to the experiences of the Anzacs.

But in Victoria in the long hot summer of 1938–39, not much public spirit was on show. Fires in state forests were not seen to be of much consequence. Fires on private property were the owner's affair. And so there were fires still burning in January which had started in October.

In 1932 FW Eggleston, a former minister in the state government, wrote despairingly of the selfish and short-sighted attitudes of the 'grazier who can get grass in the forest if he puts a fire in, and the indiscriminate settler who cuts into forest as he would into a cheese', wasting most of the timber and leaving the rest 'as fuel for fires'.

There were rural fire brigades, but these were small and uncoordinated, and had pitiful resources. One brigade listed its equipment assets as 'about four beaters and a couple of axes'. The Forests Commission had begun to develop a fire management policy, cutting fire breaks and building access roads, but it did little controlled burning to reduce the fuel load in forests under its control.

Stretton recommended the formation of a central authority able to train, coordinate and provide resources to rural volunteers. This was the genesis of the Victorian Country Fire Authority and equivalent bodies in other states, such as the Rural Fire Service. Stretton also recommended sustained education and public relations campaigns—not 'the dull lecture'—to create a new consciousness, an awareness of the danger of bushfire, and the shared responsibility of preventing it.

After Black Friday, life in the fire-prone areas of rural Australia changed. After a period of 'salvage logging'—removing dead trees before they rotted—the timber gatherers retreated from the forests. The dangerous mill settlements were abandoned; timber workers travelled further to their work from the comparative safety of towns. The mountain ash forests were emptied of people, becoming something approaching 'wilderness' for the first time in perhaps 50 000 years.

And in rural areas, fire safety became a mantra. Everyone learned how to light a fire safely, and how to put it out; about how fires behaved, and when they were most dangerous. The educational materials look ridiculous now. A poster from the 1950s shows boys and girls, dressed implausibly in their Sunday best, gravely boiling a billy: 'It is never too soon to learn to take care with fire'. But it worked. People did learn, and take care, and with time got better at living in a burning land.

But there was a great forgetting, too. Particularly in large cities, memories of the last disaster faded. In the 1960s and 1970s, the cities spread and the difference between urban and rural areas blurred. In outer suburbs and the satellite towns near large cities, people lived urban lives—but in the middle of a fire forest.

> **The sudden change, from a hot northerly to fierce squalling winds from the south-west, turned the direction of the fires. What had been a long flank became a new, raging fire front.**

ASH WEDNESDAY

The winter of 1982 was dry, with clear sunny days and bitterly cold nights. There was rain in spring—the Victorian Football League Grand Final was memorable for mud and a female streaker—but the dry weather returned over summer. In the new year a huge cloud of reddish dust, thousands of tonnes of topsoil from the Mallee, blew over the state and dimmed the sun. There were fires—in one of them, two firefighters were killed—but nothing too bad.

Then, on Wednesday 16 February 1983—Ash Wednesday in the Christian calendar—the temperature reached 40 degrees Celsius, and there was a hot north wind. Fires broke out across South Australia and Victoria, running before the wind. But it was when a cool change swept in during the afternoon that disaster really struck. The sudden change, from a hot northerly to fierce squalling winds from the south-west, turned the direction of the fires. What had been a long flank became a new, raging fire front. The temperature dropped sharply, but the fires tore through the scrub and forest and came at people who were, for the most part, utterly unprepared.

There were seventy-two deaths across Victoria and South Australia, and some 2200 houses were lost. The area burnt was very small by comparison with Black Friday, but the fires had come to where people lived. And many of those people had had little awareness of the danger.

There was a lot of anger after Ash Wednesday. People blamed local councils, firefighters, the state electricity corporation—sparks from a powerline caused one fire—the government, environmentalists. But there was also an underlying recognition, though it took time to occur, that too many people had been unprepared, and had panicked.

There was a photograph in the newspaper which became iconic: a man, wearing nothing but a pair of shorts, holding a hose. He had declared that he had fought the Japanese during World War II and that he would now fight the fire. Seconds later, the fire front had arrived. With no protection, not even a shirt, he had been killed instantly by the radiant heat.

The communities affected by Ash Wednesday learned their bitter lessons. They rebuilt, more wisely, and they have an acute awareness of fire safety to this day. Periodically since, serious fires have occurred where housing overlaps with bushland: it is what is known in official documents as 'the urban-rural interface', and which firefighters call more bluntly 'the stupid zone'. It is here that the risk of serious casualties is greatest.

In the first decade of the twenty-first century, large fires became an almost annual event in Victoria, New South Wales and the Australian Capital Territory, but they were mostly manageable. It was usually possible to protect houses and farm buildings—though there were exceptions, such as the Canberra bushfires of 2003 during which hundreds of homes were destroyed—and fatalities were rare. Despite the many deaths on Ash Wednesday, Black Friday 1939 remained Australia's great bushfire disaster.

As an historian with an interest in bushfires, I believed that the disaster of Black Friday would never be exceeded. I was wrong.

BLACK SATURDAY

At the end of his account of the 1939 fires, WS Noble wrote:

> Victoria still stands under the shadow of a great fire tragedy. If the weather conditions of Black Friday are repeated ... then all that can prevent uncontrollable fires will be the absence of serious outbreaks ... Victoria's chances of avoiding another bushfire disaster really come down to the chance of avoiding a bad fire on the wrong day, whenever it comes—as come it must.

It came.

In January and early February 2009, southern Australia wilted under what was, by most measures, the most severe heatwave in its recorded history. Across Tasmania, Victoria, South Australia and southern New South Wales, temperatures approached or exceeded the records set during January 1939.

In Melbourne, for days in succession, the maximum temperature exceeded 40 degrees Celsius. Like a stress test, the heat probed the city's infrastructure and community for weaknesses, and found them. The public transport system staggered as rails buckled and trains whose air conditioning failed became unusable because their windows didn't open. Traffic signals also failed, and the city's electricity supply struggled to cope with demand. A blanket of hot air pressed down on the city: even at dawn, the temperature did not fall much below 30 degrees Celsius.

The first week of February brought some cooler days but no rain. Already dry after a decade of drought, the state's forests were primed, a mass of potential energy set to be unleashed. Then, on Saturday 7 February, came weather from Hell.

At Hopetoun, in the Mallee, the temperature peaked at 48.8 degrees Celsius, the highest ever recorded in Victoria, or anywhere in the world this far south. The temperature in Melbourne pushed past the Black Friday record, reaching 46.4 degrees Celsius. These searing temperatures combined with very low humidity and strong winds blowing from the north, with gusts of more than 100 kilometres per hour recorded in alpine areas. And fires, at least two of them deliberately lit, tore through the Victorian countryside, hitting houses, cars and people with atomic force.

The towns of Marysville, Kinglake, Narbethong and Flowerdale were almost completely destroyed. More than 2200 houses were burnt and some 7500 people were left homeless. Thousands of animals, domestic and wild, died or were so badly burnt they had to be killed.

The destruction was immense, but what was most shocking was the number of people who died, and how.

There were those who tried to flee at the last minute and who paid horribly for doing so. At least fifteen people were killed either in their cars or near them, the vehicles blackened shells of twisted metal. But most of those who died—173 people in total, including twenty-three children—were not victims of panic. People who followed the best advice, based on the experience of decades, were incinerated in their homes. Create 'defensible space' so that your house will survive the passage of the fire front; 'stay and defend or leave early' to avoid being caught on the road—these principles work well in most places, most of the time. But they proved a death sentence for many on Black Saturday.

> **People who followed the best advice, based on the experience of decades, were incinerated in their homes.**

The intensity and speed of the Black Saturday firestorm were beyond all experience. A society which thought it knew how to handle bushfires discovered that it was wrong.

At the time of writing, a royal commission is hearing evidence. It is trying to establish how deaths might have been prevented, whether fire policy needs to change, and in what ways. Did communication break down? If so, how can this be prevented next time? Could lives have been saved in Marysville, Kinglake, Wandong? Is there anything which can protect the community from that most inexplicable evil— arson in extreme fire weather?

The commission is also there to hear people's stories, stories of death and survival, terror and confusion, horror and grief. Hearing them brings a feeling of claustrophobia, of being trapped in a feedback loop.

As Australia's foremost historian of fire, Tom Griffiths, has written:

> For those of us who know the history, the most haunting aspect of this tragedy is its familiarity. The 2009 bushfires were 1939 all over again, laced with 1983. The same images, the same stories, the same words and phrases, and the same frightening and awesome natural force that we find so hard to remember and perhaps unconsciously strive to forget.

It is not yet clear how Black Saturday will change Australia. One change may involve learning a lesson—again—from Black Friday about the value of dugouts which since the 60s have been allowed to decay and collapse. Tom Griffiths argues that in the kind of firestorm experienced on Black Saturday, the only way to escape is down: that bunkers will save lives when the next holocaust comes.

Griffiths argues that we need to re-learn a lesson from 1939: dugouts provide safe refuge in the worst fire disaster. In the decade after Black Friday, hundreds of dugouts were constructed, close at hand for anyone who lived or worked in the fire forest. But in the twenty years which followed the end of the World War II the Australian climate was kind, bringing cool temperatures and good rains. Bushfire disaster came to seem like a bad memory. Few dugouts were tested by fire. Most were allowed to decay and collapse.

It was a fatal forgetting: in extreme wildfire, the only way to escape is down.

The fires exposed the limits of experience. The people of Victoria could not know what was coming in January 1939, because, as Leonard Stretton said, 'They had not lived long enough'.

Black Saturday reminds us that we don't know as much as we think we do, and that this land is capable of the terror of the unprecedented.

During the Depression as many as one third of children in some suburbs suffered malnutrition.
(Latrobe Picture Collection, State Library of Victoria)

7

THE DEPRESSION: 1930–1939

My grandmother cleaned and kept margarine containers, and rubber bands, and the plastic bags which loaves of bread came in. She paid me pocket money to mend broken clothes pegs. In the years I knew her, she never bought a new saucepan. It was not meanness, just thrift taken to extremes.

Talking to other people about the Depression, it is astonishing how many of my grandmother's generation saved pieces of string and paper bags, and kept the dripping from the Sunday roast. It was one of the legacies of the economic calamity which swept the world in the early 1930s.

The Depression shattered the confidence and self-belief of modern industrial society. Despite World War I, in the 1920s Australia could still believe that history was a steam train, gathering pace as it powered towards a gleaming tomorrow. Prosperity would be delivered by industry and scientific agriculture, by modern government and the systems of international finance. And then, suddenly, those systems failed. Nations which thought themselves the most advanced in the world faced not just unemployment but hunger, not just political turmoil but civil collapse.

What was terrifying about the Depression was that its cause was invisible. It was not that farmers could not grow wheat, but that no-one would buy it. It was not that miners were unable to dig for coal, but that the mines had ceased production. There was coal there to be won, but no-one wanted it because the ships and trains were not working, because no-one would buy wheat at a price worth moving it for.

Working people were caught in this mystifying cycle of impoverishment—the resources were still there, their muscles and skills were still there, so why were their children going hungry?

They blamed what was called 'high finance' or 'the money power', and there was some truth to this charge. If there was an immediate cause of the Depression, it was a debt-funded speculative bubble which burst, bringing down with it banks, stockbrokers and their insurers. The bad debts rippled out into what we now know by the surreal term 'the real economy'. Businesses shut down, staff were retrenched, mortgages were foreclosed. It is grimly familiar: the current pattern of the global financial crisis.

High finance was partly responsible, then as now. But for Australia the disaster of the Depression was made far worse by the actions of governments, and political leaders were responding in large part to widely shared public opinion.

+++

Especially damaging was the idea of 'Australia Unlimited'. The phrase originated as the title of a book by Edwin Brady, published in 1918. An otherwise obscure poet, novelist and journalist, Brady argued that Australia's natural resources were literally limitless. She could become, *must* become 'the richest and most powerful ... nation of the world', a 'new United States' with a population of perhaps 100 million people.

Brady imagined the central deserts of Australia blooming with irrigated waters. The idea caught the popular imagination, and became the basis of serious policy. Perhaps in reaction to the desolation and grief of war, in the 1920s Australia entered a phase of recklessness. 'The optimists began to preach', historian Keith Hancock wrote, 'with the fervour of a tyrannical patriotism, their strange gospel'.

'Australia Unlimited' was a play on words—a contrast with private companies which are 'Limited'. The pun had unintended irony: what is 'limited' in a company is the liability of shareholders if the firm fails. Some 70 per cent of the debt taken on by Australia in the 1920s was incurred by the public sector. And the liability for these loans would indeed prove unlimited.

Public borrowing is an essential part of responsible government. This is particularly true in a nation like Australia that, at the beginning of the twenty-first century, is still being built. The catch is that the loan must be put to good use, funding something of lasting economic and social value. If not, as one economist put it, the loan becomes 'a burden as voracious as the grass hopper'. Australian governments have, since colonial times, had a tendency to borrow for grandiose or ill-judged projects. That is what occurred in Australia during the fragile prosperity of the 1920s.

The prime minister for much of this period was Stanley Melbourne Bruce. His Nationalist Party was nominally conservative, but just as it had been under Bruce's predecessor, Billy Hughes, the government was defined almost entirely by the views of its leader. And Bruce was an interventionist nation builder, ready to invest public money in development. This is not necessarily a bad thing, but most of Bruce's plans were ill-conceived, framed by the rosy worldview of Australia Unlimited. Money was spent on encouraging farming on marginal lands and developing industry behind a wall of tariff protection. In each case, the cost was high and the benefit dubious—but credit was easy.

Like the other dominion nations of the British Empire, Australia enjoyed privileged status as a borrower in London. We were given loans at low interest, and needed to provide little in the way of security. The intent was to strengthen the bonds of Empire, but Australia abused the privilege. In the period 1925–28, Australia accounted for 43 per cent of the total of British lending. The borrowing continued as the decade wore on, even when other dominions could see difficult economic times ahead and began to reign in their spending. Between July 1927 and July 1928, Australian governments borrowed more than £63 million in ten separate loans. In the five years to 1928, the interest burden on Australian loans rose from £19 million to almost £28 million, an increase of 44 per cent.

The government of New South Wales was a big borrower. There, politics was a revolving door; Nationalist and Labor administrations came and went—one held government for only twelve hours. However, with the support of Labor leader Jack Lang, when he was both in and out of government, an ambitious program of public works went ahead. The giant of these was JJC Bradfield's plan for an underground city railway and the Sydney Harbour Bridge. Lang, who became premier in 1925, arranged for a high-powered delegation to visit London to raise funds for the Bradfield Plan—a staggering total of more than £43 million.

There were many voices raised in warning. John Maynard Keynes was one critic: he saw little productive benefit from the loans. A London broking firm said in a report: 'In the whole of the British Empire there is no more voracious borrower than the Australian Commonwealth. Loan follows loan with disconcerting frequency ... they get the money they want when they want it'.

> 'In the whole of the British Empire there is no more voracious borrower than the Australian Commonwealth.'

And there were warnings in Australia, too. Economist Edward Shann repeatedly argued that the idea of 'protection all round', based on a 'fair' price, was simply unsustainable: 'It deranges and weakens its whole economy'. He warned that only high commodity prices kept the whole creaking edifice from collapse.

In 1927 Shann published a pamphlet, 'a call to Australia to put her house in order lest drought and falling prices for wool and wheat overtake us again'. No-one paid much attention, but two years later the prices for wool and wheat tumbled, and Australia plunged into crisis.

COLLAPSE

In the wake of the 1929 Wall Street stock market crash, the prices of commodities dived. In less than three years, the unit value of Australian exports had been halved. It was impossible to increase production enough to make up the difference, even had buyers been available.

Export income fell from £645 million to £460 million in two years—a decline of 30 per cent. Inevitably, Australia's balance of trade fell sharply into deficit. In 1929–30, the current account deficit was £72 million pounds—a colossal figure for a nation of just 6 million people. Meanwhile, the massive debts that had been taken on still had to be serviced. The state and federal governments were forced to run rapidly increasing budget deficits.

With export income slashed and a crippling external debt burden, the Australian protection economy—built around high wages and costs sheltered by tariffs—was extremely vulnerable. Businesses slid into bankruptcy, the bad debts and cancelled orders dragging others down. Workers were laid off, demand slumped further: it was a savage downward spiral.

Economic crisis brought political crisis. Triumphantly elected in 1929, the federal Labor government of James Scullin found itself trapped in a nightmare. The economic collapse was so severe that there were genuine fears of food riots, of the breakdown of civil order, of armed conflict.

The misery and fear of the Depression in Australia have faded from memory, partly because we know what happened next: that collapse was averted, and that liberal democracy survived. In large part because the experience of the Depression drove the creation of the welfare system, we also fail to understand the sharpest pain of that experience: hunger.

It is difficult to accurately gauge unemployment during the Depression. It had already been high in 1928, at nearly 11 per cent of union members; at its peak in 1932 it was 29 per cent. These figures were collected by trade unions, which only counted unemployment among their members. While rates of union membership were high, there were still large numbers of people who did not belong to a union. There was also informal part-time work, the jobs of women and older children, which did not show up in trade union figures. Historian Michael Cannon suggests that the true rate of unemployment was more than double the official rate—perhaps even higher if you include the many workers who were reduced to working one or two days per week.

The dry economic figures, astonishing though they are, do not capture fully the extent of the social trauma which the Depression wrought on Australia. There were those for whom times were lean but who got by. For people who kept their jobs, wages fell by as much as 20 per cent—an austerity measure introduced under what was called the Premiers' Plan. But the cost of living fell sharply as well, and those in this situation, working perhaps for the public service or a large company, could consider themselves fortunate.

People running small business and farms often faced bankruptcy. Even more vulnerable were unskilled working-class people, already poor and often with large families and few assets.

The unemployed were entitled to 'sustenance', often called 'susso' or the dole. Schemes varied from state to state, but a typical dole was 9 shillings and 6 pence per week for a single adult, more for families. The dole was paid in the form of coupons which could be exchanged for food at a butcher or grocer—not, however, greengrocers, so fresh fruit and vegetables were hard to obtain. For most families, the dole would provide enough food for about three days. For the rest of the week, it was what could be grown, what might be provided by private charities, or what could be scrounged.

Thousands of people were unable to pay rent or keep up mortgage repayments and were left homeless. Shantytowns sprang up on vacant land around the cities and towns. The most famous of these encampments was Happy Valley near La Perouse in Sydney's south, close to the mouth of Botany Bay. People used scrap timber, flattened kerosene tins, hessian sacks and whatever else they could find to build some sort of shelter. Lady Gwendolen Game, wife of the governor of New South Wales, visited Happy Valley in June 1931. She estimated that about 350 families, 1000 people in all, were living there, subsisting entirely on the food dole.

People used scrap timber, flattened kerosene tins, hessian sacks and whatever else they could find to build some sort of shelter.

Mick Masson, who travelled through the eastern states during the Depression, saw many such camps. They sprang up on rifle ranges, in showgrounds, in nature reserves. Around Newcastle, where unemployment was particularly bad, there were several camps, some built on poles above tidal estuaries. Wherever there was the possibility of work—fruit picking, or loading and unloading trains, labouring on the wharfs—communities of unemployed men would form, sleeping wherever they could find shelter.

Many of these camps were on low-lying ground, and without adequate drainage they became fetid. Lice and dysentery were common, and many children suffered from whooping cough. Masson reported seeing people suffering from scurvy, and bitterly remembered the stench caused by the disease.

In Melbourne, the most visible dole camp was Dudley Flats, a corrugated-iron shantytown between a busy railway line and the docks. There were similar camps in Adelaide and Perth. Many remained for years, only being demolished and their occupants rehoused in the late 1930s.

Even among those who were able to keep their homes, deprivation was often acute. Infant mortality in the Melbourne slum of Fitzroy in 1932 was eighty per 1000 births—more than twice the rate in more affluent suburbs, and higher than in modern Bangladesh. In 1934 a Melbourne city health officer reported that 34 per cent of the children seen by him were suffering malnutrition.

The newspapers reported—often almost in passing—even worse stories. In September 1934, a coroner's court heard that a woman in Wagga had killed her own baby and then died herself because of hunger and neglect. Alma Burnett, aged nineteen, was found lying on the floor of her bedroom. There was no food in the house, and the only furniture was a bed with an old mattress and no blankets. Burnett's baby, born that morning, had been strangled. Burnett was taken to Wagga District Hospital, but she later died.

+ + +

Considering such desperate times, it is easy to understand the electoral appeal of Jack Lang, the Labor premier of New

South Wales, during the early years of the Depression. A big man, tall and physically dominating, with a jutting jaw and heavy brow, Lang had a raw, effective speaking style. He would roar: 'While there is a pinched and starving belly in Balmain, not a penny, not a penny, to the bloated bondholders in London'. If you were a union man, out of work and angry, it was what you wanted to hear.

The dominant view of Jack Lang today is one promoted by a Lang protégé who went on to become a Labor prime minister: Paul Keating. By this view, when hard times had come, Lang, the People's Champion, was the one who had stood up to the British banks. It is a surprise, then, to learn that most of Lang's Labor contemporaries detested him. He was seen as a divisive egotist who, through his reckless posturing, had split the Labor Party and brought New South Wales to the brink of collapse.

To be fair, Lang was unfortunate in winning government for the second time just as economic disaster struck. The financial crisis in New South Wales was acute. As early as November 1930, Lang's correspondence reveals a desperate situation: £2 million due Monday next, another £1.5 million on 15 December, interest payment of £1.3 million to be made in London on 1 January. The state government simply did not have the money, and the banks were reluctant to advance credit. 'My particular anxiety', he wrote to the federal treasurer, 'is to find means of obtaining the necessary cash to carry on during the months of December and January'.

With such large and growing numbers of people unemployed, state agencies faced unprecedented strain. The problems facing Lang's government were immense, and his proposals were not as radical as his rhetoric made them sound. However, that very rhetoric was grossly irresponsible. By needlessly antagonising the business sector and by inflaming the fears of the middle class, Lang took his state to the brink of civil conflict.

In May 1931, the federal and state governments met in Melbourne to thrash out a response to the crisis. The plan that was adopted followed the stern prescription of Sir Otto Neimeyer, a representative of the Bank of England—one of Australia's major creditors—who had been sent to Australia to advise the federal government. Neimeyer had recommended cuts to award wages, balanced government budgets and no further overseas borrowing until short-term debt was repaid.

The rhetoric of the Premiers' Plan, as it was called, was that of 'equality of sacrifice'—we have all been living beyond our means and must reduce our standard of living to a sustainable level. This fiscal discipline had the effect of further contracting the economy, and probably made the Depression worse. However, the premiers were following the economic orthodoxy of the day—and they had little option, as any hope of recovery and spending their way out of the crisis depended on continued access to credit.

In 1931, Lang announced that the interest due to English banks would not be paid. In order to preserve Australian creditworthiness, the federal government was forced to meet the debt. By August, the situation in New South Wales was desperate—the government was unable to pay the salaries of public servants—and after making some concessions to the other states, Lang was granted an emergency loan.

But Lang's rhetoric became increasingly wild. He linked the issue of loan repayments to Australian war casualties, declaring: 'The same people who conscripted our sons and laid them in Flanders' fields ... now demand more blood, the interest on their lives'. This emotive claim was misleading. Total Australian public debt stood at £1.1 *billion*, and only 16 per cent of Australia's overseas repayments were war-related. By far the bulk of the debt had been taken on in the 1920s for grandiose public works, including a huge loan incurred by Lang's government for the construction of the Sydney Harbour Bridge.

+ + +

Australian society reacted to the Depression with confusion and anger, and searched for someone to blame. 'Something ... must be done to prevent us finishing in the economic necropolis', mused RH Milford. 'True statesmanship and co-operation will achieve this; and the present party-system must be thrown away—root and branch.' Such antidemocratic sentiments were widely shared. Essington Lewis, the general manager of BHP, wrote that ruling by democracy 'seems to be an unmitigated disaster', and that a short-lived dictatorship 'would not be altogether a bad thing for Australia'.

It was in this situation of turmoil and widespread fear that the New Guard arose, the closest thing Australia has had to a fascist movement. The New Guard is mostly remembered for one of its members, Captain Francis de Groot, who on horseback and dressed in a cavalry uniform, crashed the opening ceremony of the Sydney Harbour Bridge on 19 March 1932. Having cut the ribbon, de Groot raised his sword, declaring: 'In the name of the decent citizens of New South Wales, I declare this bridge open'. De Groot's piece of theatre is often presented as amusing but unimportant, a schoolboy prank at Lang's expense. But de Groot's words and actions directly challenged constitutional government. He was appealing to patriotic tradition while calling for direct action. As one supporter wrote to de Groot, the time had come when 'fascism, with modifications, should take an active form in Australia'.

It is almost certain that some elements of the New Guard seriously contemplated a coup. It is unlikely they would have succeeded, but in 1932 the New Guard was a powerful organisation, with 80 000 members. They had mounted a campaign of violence against communists and other left-wing political groups, and were considered by the police as a serious threat to public order.

Lang continued his brinkmanship. After he had defaulted on debt repayments, the federal government passed legislation allowing it to seize state revenues for the repayments. Lang responded by withdrawing more than £1 million in cash from state government bank accounts. He had it stored in the State Treasury, guarded by unemployed unionists. Public servants were instructed to conduct all transactions in cash and to disobey the federal government.

As the political crisis deepened, the governor of New South Wales, Sir Philip Game, sacked Lang as premier on

13 May 1932. Game's action was constitutionally suspect, but justified by the very real prospect of civil violence.

With a change of government, the New Guard faded from prominence. Australia's only real flirtation with fascism had failed.

RESCUE

The widespread disillusionment and disgust with politics caused by the Depression was understandable, but it was also destructive. Crisis requires leadership, engagement and an acceptance of responsibility. There was not much of any of these qualities evident in the early 1930s.

James Scullin's federal Labor government was unequal to the task. Distintegrating under the pressure, it was brought down. Federal parliament was, for a time, in disarray, with six different parties in the House of Representatives. This was, in some ways, an accurate reflection of the nation as a whole, whose political and economic leadership was floundering.

Rescue came in the unlikely form of the United Australia Party (UAP). Formed as an emergency coalition of conservative politicians and Labor defectors, the UAP lasted less than ten years and was always a strained alliance of interests. But federally under Prime Minister Joe Lyons, and in New South Wales under Premier Bertram Stevens, the UAP was vital to Australia's recovery from the Depression.

Stevens, in particular, deserves to be better remembered. Coming to power at a time of crisis, he restored stability to the basic institutions of state. Stevens had the dull virtues of the Methodist lay preacher and the upright Treasury official he had been before entering politics, but these were exactly what were needed at the time. He was fiscally disciplined, but was able to resist pressure from business interests to balance the Budget at the expense of unemployment relief. For the people of New South Wales, while long, hard and bitter years remained, the threat of social collapse had been averted.

Lyons and Stevens were leaders of the sort historian Manning Clark derided as having the 'virtues of receivers in bankruptcy'. But there is something to be said for such virtues, particularly when the state is bankrupt. Their stewardship was necessary for Australia's economic recovery—an achingly slow process which was not fully complete when another world war began in 1939.

Crisis requires leadership, engagement and an acceptance of responsibility. There was not much of any of these qualities evident in the early 1930s.

'HERMIT AUSTRALIA'

For decades after the Depression, Australia was marked by caution and an excessive reluctance to take risks. The Depression generation came to value security, especially job security, to an extent which stifled initiative and innovation. Safety lay with the government department, the state-owned monopoly and the large company—preferably one like an airline or television station which was protected from competition by regulation. We became ever more wedded to a reflexive protectionism that extended well beyond economics to popular culture and intellectual life.

In 1938, the 150th anniversary of British settlement in Australia, the *Women's Weekly* published a famous front cover in which Australia was personified as a young woman in a white dress: cheerful, healthy and active, with white teeth and a slight tan. She was innocent, pure, carefree.

But if Australia was a girl in white, she led a very sheltered life. Immigration restrictions designed to preserve White Australia—'Nothing against them, but you wouldn't want her to *marry* one'—were just one facet of a culture of protectionism. She was protected by tariffs, from 'unfair' competition, by extensive censorship from films that might upset or embarrass her, by customs officers from corrupting books.

The economic historian Edward Shann had identified this malaise as early as 1930: 'The more the policy of hermit Australia succeeded, the more surely would it bring slothful intellectual standards, and, as a consequence, material decay'.

Even the shock of World War II could not completely shake Hermit Australia. While learning to live in a world of atomic weapons and antagonistic superpowers, a world in which the British Empire was a fading ghost and Asia was rising, protectionism remained dogma. Australia wanted protection from Japanese-made cars, from coloured migrants, from copies of *Lady Chatterley's Lover*, from dangerous ideas.

Ironically, as the world emerged from the war and Hermit Australia thought again of nation building, it did so by reviving its most dangerous idea: Edwin Brady's 'Australia Unlimited'. This time, we called it the Snowy Mountains Scheme.

Building a pressure tunnel, part of the vast Snowy Mountains Scheme. The Snowy was a source of pride. So were the Pyramids. (Latrobe Picture Collection, State Library of Victoria)

8
THE GREAT WHITE ELEPHANT: THE SNOWY MOUNTAINS SCHEME, 1949–1974

Because of its rarity and striking appearance, the albino elephant was considered sacred in ancient Siam, a symbol of the emperor's power and semi-divine nature. One emperor devised an ingenious way to punish any prince who annoyed him: he would present the man with one of the sacred white elephants. The gift could not possibly be refused, nor given away, and keeping the elephant in the magnificent style which custom demanded would financially ruin even the wealthiest of nobles.

This story is the origin of the expression 'white elephant', meaning a splendid, high-status possession which is not particularly productive, costs a lot to maintain, and which you cannot get rid of. Since colonial times, Australians have had a weakness for white elephants. We are endlessly willing to build big, running up staggering debts to construct railways, dams and bridges, more for reasons of status than utility.

+ + +

The Depression put all thought of major capital works on hold for more than a decade. But even before the end of World War II, Australian leaders were again thinking big.

Australia emerged from the war in a far better economic position than it had been in thirty years earlier. The country had returned to full employment. It had borrowed heavily to fund the war effort, but mostly from its own people through war bonds. Commodity prices were strong and the economy had grown, so external loans could be serviced without great difficulty. During the war, the federal government had been given the power to levy an income tax, and so had a strong financial base.

With only 7 million people and a small industrial base, Australia felt vulnerable.

Peacetime brought an opportunity for nation building, for creating a more-just society in which prosperity could be better shared. Australia was conscious, too, of being a small country in a world which had recently experienced two devastating wars. The fall of Singapore in 1942 had confirmed what World War I should have taught us: that the British Empire was not a source of security. With only 7 million people and a small industrial base, Australia felt vulnerable. We needed more people, and a more diverse economy.

Herbert Cole Coombs, or 'Nugget' as he was universally known, emerged as the most influential figure in postwar reconstruction. He feared the disillusionment that often follows war, when the spirit of self-sacrifice and unity of purpose turns into cynicism and apathy. At a high-level conference held in Canberra in January 1944, Coombs said that what was needed was a Great Project:

> Men do derive personal satisfaction from major constructional achievements. One only has to think of the satisfaction of New

Southwelshmen in the Sydney Bridge [or] the pride of the Russians in the Dnieper Dam.

Coombs was referring to the massive Lenin Dam, more than 750 metres across, built on the Dnieper River in modern Ukraine in the 1930s. This dam was the star project of Stalin's first Five Year Plan, a program of breakneck industrialisation which came at massive economic and human cost.

Coombs went on:

Perhaps even the slaves who toiled and sweated in the construction of the Pyramids derived some satisfaction from their grandeur. The more complex triumphs [of] modern engineering [inspire] a real, if vicarious, sense of power and achievement.

Whether slavery and Stalinism provide the ideal blueprint for nation building is debatable. But it was this spirit which lay behind the Snowy Mountains Scheme, often simply called 'the Snowy', and Coombs got the psychology right. Alistair Mant, who worked on the Snowy as a young man, recalled that the 'most important thing about the Snowy Mountains Project, in the drab years following World War II, is that it was big, exciting and important'.

The idea of damming rivers that rose on the eastern side of the Great Dividing Range and channelling them inland had a long pedigree. JJC Bradfield, the man behind the Sydney Harbour Bridge, was an early proponent. In the late 1930s, he envisaged diverting the rivers of northern Queensland to the interior. The Dead Heart would bloom:

from Alice Springs to Birdsville, the land would support sheep and cattle, rice and cotton, maize and wheat, tea and tropical fruits.

Even earlier, in 1880, there had been suggestions that the waters of the Snowy River, in southern New South Wales, could be diverted inland into the Murrumbidgee River. Nothing came of it at the time, but in the wake of World War II the Snowy River's moment arrived.

Labor Prime Minister Ben Chifley shared Coombs' concerns about postwar morale and his enthusiasm for nation-building. In a radio broadcast in January 1949, he announced the Snowy Mountains Scheme as a 'plan for a nation', one that would cost £185 million and take a generation to complete. The project, it was claimed, would provide hydro-electricity at half the cost of coal-fired power stations.

The Snowy was seen as a vote winner for the Labor government, which faced a tough election late in 1949, so the project was 'started' as soon as possible, in October. Only one person had been appointed to the Snowy Mountains Authority: its commissioner, William Hudson. But in a ceremony staged for the newsreel cameras, Australia's governor-general detonated some explosives and declared that the 'work' had begun.

The leader of the opposition Liberal Party, Robert Menzies, had boycotted this pointless explosion, and when Labor lost government in December the project's future was uncertain. However, when in government, Menzies was won over. This happened partly because of the scheme's popularity, and partly because of pressure from the politically powerful Murrumbidgee irrigators. Another factor was the rabbit-proof fence syndrome: the Australian tendency to want to finish things even if they should never have been started.

The sheer magnitude of the Snowy Mountains Scheme is difficult to convey. The eventual cost of the project, £422 million, was greater than the entire annual tax revenue of all state and territory governments in 1947. In contemporary terms, it was the equivalent of embarking on a project that would cost more than $200 billion. Of course, all of the money was not needed at once, and the economy and tax revenue were expected to grow, which they did. Even so, the Snowy represented a staggering investment.

William Hudson, who was in charge of the project for almost two decades, was one of Australia's great engineers. A veteran of several big hydro-electric projects, he had a reputation for getting them built on time and on budget. Many of his workers were migrants who had been displaced by the political division of Europe after World War II. Hudson made a success of the most ethnically diverse workforce Australia had seen. 'You'll be neither Slavs nor Balts', he told one group of potential workers, 'but men of the Snowy'. Some 100 000 migrants from thirty different nations worked on the scheme during the twenty-five years of its construction—many consequently established themselves in Australia. When it was finally completed in 1974, ahead of schedule, the cost was close to what had been budgeted.

The sheer magnitude of the Snowy Mountains Scheme is difficult to convey.

It was—and still is—awesome. There are sixteen dams and seven power stations. The water is channelled along 80 kilometres of aqueducts and through 145 kilometres of tunnels, many blasted through solid rock. The scheme's combined storage capacity is equal to that of every dam and reservoir built in Australia before 1940. It has been recognised internationally as an Industrial Wonder of the World, and placed on the National Heritage Register.

Clever public relations and astutely managed media coverage portrayed the Snowy as a great national enterprise, a practical and pragmatic scheme that would help Australia grow. And it is as an icon, an object of pride, that the Snowy looms largest in the public consciousness. 'Frankly', runs a typical newspaper headline, 'this is Australia's finest work'. Alistair Mant believes that, 'in some ways, the Snowy Mountains Scheme *made* Australia'.

> **'Pride became the Snowy spirit and Australia has walked tall ever since.'**

Historian Brad Collis calls the Snowy Australia's 'rite of passage' as a modern nation: 'It cut the apron strings with Mother England and transformed a narrow, farm-based economy into that of an advanced industrial nation ... Pride became the Snowy spirit and Australia has walked tall ever since'.

In the face of such passion, it seems bad-mannered to question the Snowy. But the whole scheme was misconceived from the start, persevered with despite repeated warnings of its drawbacks. It was the result of one of Australia's most dangerous delusions.

THE 50-ACRE FUTURE

The Snowy is the most costly outcome of the dream of Australia Unlimited, Edwin Brady's fantasy of a blooming inland. Brady prophesied a mighty Australia with millions of people supported by massive irrigation schemes: 'There are on our inland rivers strips of fertile red soil ... still awaiting with the thirst of centuries for these fertilizing waters which will convert their arid miles into Arabian gardens of perfume and delight'.

The backbone of this mighty work would be the small farmer. Touring the irrigation areas, Brady

> saw SUCCESS written in large letters ... the writer found new settlers on 20-acre blocks making a good living. One family started with less than £20 in cash, and within a few months sold £150 of produce ... *The 50-acre farmers are the men of the future in Australia*. [original emphasis]

Brady's daydream became conventional wisdom. A school textbook from the 1920s reflects the spirit of the age: 'More than half the large area of Australia ... is arid or semi-arid ... Yet the land will give splendid returns if only water can be provided for it'. The best way to do this? 'There is still an enormous amount of water which rushes each year from the mountains to the sea' and which could be diverted to 'the arid and unprofitable parts of Australia'. This would allow 'Closer Settlement', the ideal of settling 'many more men on the land by dividing up large estates into smaller blocks, well watered, for intensive irrigation'.

The small farm has a special place in the Australian heart. The celebration of the farmer, tough and independent, the rock upon which the Australian nation is built, has survived beyond all reason.

For decades, well into the 1960s, social reformers saw the small farm as offering both economic and moral redemption for the urban poor. In CJ Dennis' mock epic *The Sentimental Bloke*, the larrikin hero ends up married and settled on a farm, an "ealthy, 'appy, 'ardy son o' toil'. The smoking, cursing street fighter is reborn

> *frum the ashes of a ne'er-do-well*
> *A bloomin' farmer's blossimin' like 'ell*

Very often there was more hell in small farming than Dennis realised.

In the decades leading up to World War I, governments tried, time after time, to promote closer settlement. Millions of pounds were spent purchasing land, building roads and railways, and in start-up loans to would-be farmers. Even more was spent constructing the huge dams which would supply the water to make the dream possible. And time after time the effort failed.

The saddest attempt at closer settlement was the Soldier Settlement Scheme created in the wake of World War I. Focusing on the already troubled Murrumbidgee Irrigation Area, the scheme advanced almost £50 million (mostly borrowed) to some 37 000 returned soldiers to take up farms. Many had no experience in farming. The farms were too small to support a family, even in full production and given favourable seasons. Long before the Depression and the commodity price crash, one-third of the returned soldiers had abandoned their farms. Half the money loaned had been written off.

Soldier settlement was an economic and social disaster: a plan based on a sentimental idea which squandered public money and tangled thousands of families in debt, useless toil and suffering.

In Australia, we have a peculiar twin fetish: we love small things, especially small farms. But we also love big things. It is remarkable how many things in Australia are called 'Great': the Barrier Reef, the Australian Bight, the line of tallish hills which forms the Dividing Range, the Artesian Basin. In Melbourne, one half of a big sports stadium is called the Great Southern Stand. Australia also has the Big Banana, the Big Pineapple and many other paeans to bigness.

> And such was the perceived merit of small farmers populating the countryside that almost any cost, any inefficiency, any absurdity could be justified

A large irrigation dams fits both bills because it is a big thing that helps the small farm. And such was the perceived merit of small farmers populating the countryside that almost any cost, any inefficiency, any absurdity could be justified to support them.

The Snowy Mountains Scheme took this philosophy to new heights. It generated electricity, but at a far greater cost than conventional power stations. If there was a justification for the scheme, it was to provide water for inland irrigation. But not one irrigation project in Australia's history had ever recovered the cost of construction, and the Snowy would be the most expensive scheme yet attempted. Even in the early stages of planning, there was no pretence that the irrigation component would be economically viable. Even so, a parliamentary committee was adamant that, regardless of cost, 'requirements of irrigation and stock and domestic [water] supplies should ... in the national interest have first call on the sources of the Snowy River'.

Any investment, particularly a large one which draws on scarce resources, must be justified in terms of what economists call 'opportunity cost'. If we commit to this investment, are we missing out on other, better opportunities? Could our capital, materials and labour be better used elsewhere?

+++

By this measure, the Snowy cannot be justified. There were a host of important infrastructure needs in Australia at the end of World War II. Investment was needed in roads and public transport, in hospitals and kindergartens, in schools and universities, in ports and civilian air transport, in the telephone system and in broadcasting. Such basic needs as clean water and sewerage were lacking in many country towns and outer city suburbs. There was a chronic shortage of housing, especially low-cost housing, all over Australia.

In postwar Australia, the Snowy Mountains Scheme was a giant succubus.

The Snowy drained resources from these far worthier public works. It diminished the nation's wealth and lowered its standard of living. In postwar Australia, the Snowy Mountains Scheme was a giant succubus.

It was not just an economic disaster, but a social and environmental disaster as well. For decades, much of the irrigation water was used unwisely and inefficiently—not least because the cost was massively subsidised—resulting in salinity and land degradation. And so much water was diverted that the Snowy River itself was all but destroyed. By the 1990s, the flow of the river's upper reaches had been reduced to 1 per cent of its natural volume. This was not enough to keep the river channel clear of vegetation and silt, and the breeding grounds of fish were disrupted or destroyed. With such low volume, the polluting effect of run-off was more severe: algal blooms became a regular summer event. Where the Snowy River meets the sea, at Marlo in Victoria, salt water pushed up to 10 kilometres further inland, damaging farmland on the surrounding floodplain. A campaign to restore the river to reasonable health with the release of extra water was successful, but only after a long struggle.

Meanwhile, along the inland rivers, a social tragedy unfolded. Irrigation was allowed to expand far beyond sustainable limits. State governments allocated water licences which consumed more water than the river system could provide. By the mid 1980s, irrigated agriculture was already in crisis. Experts recommended that water had to be priced at something approaching its true cost, and that farmers take a more responsible attitude to the resource.

People tried, but unscrambling the omelette of Australian irrigation was difficult. Each attempted reform seemed to produce a new absurd anomaly: farmers paying for water they didn't use, or profitably on-selling 'rights' to water that had never existed.

There was plenty of warning that Australia's rivers were under stress. Most spectacularly, in November 1991 the

Darling River turned bright blue for almost 1000 kilometres. It was a bloom of toxic blue-green algae, the largest recorded in any river anywhere in the world.

When, at the turn of the new century, the most severe drought since Federation hit Australia, the overtaxed rivers approached the point of failure. Farmers were restricted to less and less of their water quotas: down to half, then 30 per cent, then to 15 per cent, and in some cases to almost nothing. The result: doomed orchards that were bulldozed and burnt, crops that failed or were not planted at all, bankruptcies, suicides, families breaking up—anger, bitter recrimination, social disintegration. It was Soldier Settlement all over again, but on a bigger scale.

And it should never have happened.

In 1963, an agricultural economist, writing anonymously, warned that every irrigation scheme yet attempted had led to shattered hopes and bad debts:

> The truth is that irrigation abounds in economic and social problems ... These demand very detailed and critical study before large sums of capital are invested ... It would be better to allow Snowy water to flow out to sea than to use it wastefully and uneconomically.

How much economic loss, damaged land and heartache could have been avoided if we had listened?

Perhaps the richest irony of the whole Snowy story occurred in 2006. The federal, New South Wales and Victorian governments, joint owners of the scheme, decided to privatise it, floating it on the Australian Stock Exchange. There was a howl of public protest. So strong was the revolt that the federal government, which had already sold half of Telstra, Qantas, the Commonwealth Bank and a host of other key enterprises, relented. Then Prime Minister John Howard said: 'There is an overwhelming feeling in the community that the Snowy is an icon ... part of the great saga of post-World War II reconstruction'.

The decision was a major embarrassment to the state governments, who had already budgeted the proceeds of the sale towards unspectacular but important public works.

The failed privatisation confirms the Snowy as a true white elephant. We can't even sell the bloody thing.

1976 was a bad year for Australian swimmers, and for Australian swimwear.
(National Archives of Australia: A6180, 17/3/76/3)

9
FOOL'S GOLD: THE MONTREAL OLYMPIC GAMES, 1976

Australia's athletes set off for the Olympic Games in Canada in July 1976 in what were, even for the 1970s, horrible uniforms, but with high hopes. We had done well in Munich four years earlier, winning eight gold and seventeen medals overall, placing us sixth on the medal tally.

'Optimistically', wrote journalist Ron Carter, 'our men and women could come home with 29 medals. Of course, if things go badly for us ... only a handful will come Australia's way'. The standard of international competition had risen, so Australians would 'do well just to get to the finals in Montreal. But then, who wants to know a finalist? The only Olympians who get a pat on the back are those with a medal'.

This was not how things were supposed to be. 'The important thing in the Olympic games is not to win, but to take part', said the founder of the modern games, Pierre de Coubertin, adding:

> The important thing in life is not the triumph but the struggle. The essential thing is not to have conquered but to have fought well. To spread these precepts is to build up a stronger, a more valiant and above all a more scrupulous and more generous humanity.

The International Olympic Committee (IOC) pretends to embrace this ideal, posting medal tallies that are 'for information only', as it 'does not recognise global ranking per country'. But Ron Carter was merely acknowledging the truth: for most competing nations, winning is everything.

And in Montreal, we did not win.

The team, almost 200-strong, brought back one silver medal. Even that felt like a loss because it was in the men's hockey, in which gold and silver are decided in a play-off. There were four bronze medals: two in yachting, one in an equestrian event, and one in swimming.

> 'Optimistically', wrote journalist Ron Carter, 'our men and women could come home with 29 medals. Of course, if things go badly for us … only a handful will come Australia's way'.

It was in the pool, where Australia had long been a power, that the disappointment rankled the most. As the tournament unfolded, continual failure led to bitter recriminations. One headline captured the catfight: 'Lean day for our "fat" girls'. The sole swimming medal was won by Stephen Holland in the 1500 metres freestyle. Holland swam a personal-best time, but this admirable achievement produced the headline 'Goldless Games?' and this summary of the swimming competition: 'One bronze medal and a lot of disappointment'.

Australia finished in thirty-second place on the medal table. First, with forty-nine gold, was the Soviet Union. Third, with thirty-four gold, was the United States. And sandwiched between the two superpowers, with forty gold, twenty-five silver and twenty-five bronze medals, was the GDR.

'The *what*?', anyone under the age of thirty-five is likely to ask. To explain, it is helpful to look at some old postage stamps.

My daughter recently took up stamp collecting. Helping her sort her collection was like stepping through a time warp. If you don't think the world has changed much since 1976, try explaining to a 7-year-old what the Soviet Union was. There are all these huge, colourful stamps from communist countries which no longer exist: satellites and cosmonauts, smiling peasants with their new tractors, and lots of Olympic athletes. These were idealised, modernist forms of men and women, with layered slabs of muscle: they hurled disks and hammers and javelins; rode bicycles, rowed, sprinted, swam—they were physically perfect incarnations of a socialist paradise.

The Cold War was symbolically fought out in the stadiums of the Olympic Games. Successful athletes were somehow thought to validate the political systems which trained them. And the communists were—there was no denying it—good at sport. The Soviet Union always topped the Olympic medal tally. And right up there with the giants was the oddity 'GDR'— the German Democratic Republic, or East Germany.

This country emerged in 1945 from that part of the defeated Third Reich that had ended up under Soviet control. Of all the nations of the Communist bloc, East Germany struggled most for legitimacy. The poor cousin of an artificially divided people, its survival dependent on Soviet tanks, it had to build walls to keep its own people in. It is not hard to see why a shabby little police state with image issues strove for sporting success. Gold medals were an assertion of excellence and efficiency, a claim to genuine nationhood.

The East German system for identifying and training talent in elite sports, the 'medal factory', was astonishing in its effectiveness. From Munich in 1972 to Seoul in 1988, this nation of only 17 million people won 384 medals. It finished second in the medal tally three times.

They were, of course, cheating a lot of the time. Between 8000 and 9000 East German athletes were given performance-enhancing drugs in the period between 1972 and the collapse of the regime in 1989. The main drug administered was the 'blue bean', Oral-Turinabol, an anabolic steroid containing testosterone. The drug greatly improved an athlete's recovery time and boosted muscle build-up, but it also had horrific side effects: female infertility, male testicular cancer, breast cancer and heart disease. About one in ten East German athletes was left with a serious illness.

However, the revelations of systematic doping obscured a deeper truth. Some of the coaches involved in the doping said: 'We felt legitimized by state policy ... our prime task was to achieve international success, notably by winning medals'. The blue bean was just one aspect of this poisonous system. The medal factory took sport and twisted it into a sickly obsession: a grim state religion, to which health and youth were sacrificed.

'LEARN FROM THE EAST GERMANS'

The 1976 Montreal Olympic Games were a disaster, not because our athletes performed poorly, but because of how our society responded to the poor performances. There was an unmistakable sense of national shame. The media agonised: 'Where did we go wrong?' Montreal caused a 'crisis for the Government', and debate raged over how Australia could 'regain its lost athletic potency'.

The success of East Germany was particularly galling because its population was similar in size to that of Australia. One journalist declared: 'We have hit rock bottom as a swimming nation ... and it could take us 16 years to get back up again with the East Germans'. This prediction was remarkably accurate. By the time the 1992 Barcelona Olympics took place, Australia was again emerging as a swimming power, while East Germany no longer existed.

Until the late 1970s, Australia had managed to combine a tradition of amateur sport with an obsessive desire to win. But Montreal forced a choice. Do we continue to treasure our liberal traditions, our laid-back and democratic temper? Or do we want to win? The answer was consciously to imitate the East German medal factory.

The awkward fact that East Germany was a communist dictatorship caused defensiveness. 'If we are to learn from the East Germans', declared the *Sydney Morning Herald*, 'we need to look at their sports system rather than their political system'. There was a slight hitch in this argument. If poor Australian performances reflected badly on us as a nation, East German sporting success to some extent must have vindicated the culture and political system which produced it. Despite this contradiction and the initial coolness of Liberal Prime

Minister Malcolm Fraser, support for an elite sports training program along East German lines gradually grew.

The 1980 Olympics, held in Moscow, were another debacle for Australia. The government unsuccessfully 'encouraged' a boycott over the Soviet invasion of Afghanistan, which led to a reduced team that was not allowed to carry the Australian flag at the opening ceremony. We performed better than at Montreal but even so, the row over participation was politically embarrassing. Something was needed to bring the sports establishment back on side. On 26 January 1981—Australia Day— the once-sceptical Fraser officially opened the Australian Institute of Sport (AIS) in Canberra.

In the decades since, the AIS has expanded massively, supported by successive federal governments. It now has a national network of sports institutes and academies. These centres provide training programs for thousands of athletes in twenty-five sports. The AIS is seen as a tremendous national success. Kevan Gosper, a senior IOC official, described it as 'a shrine of excellence ... one of Australia's more successful ventures in education and research. You have to have an icon for excellence in sport, and that is the AIS'.

There is a lot of talk of excellence surrounding elite sport. To excel means to be superior to another, to surpass them—to *win*. And it is presented as an unquestioned virtue.

There is a lot of talk of excellence surrounding elite sport. To excel means to be superior to another, to surpass them—to *win*. And it is presented as an unquestioned virtue.

The AIS was soon dubbed the 'gold medal factory'. Australia won four gold medals in Los Angeles in 1984; five in Seoul, 1988; seven in Barcelona, 1992; nine in Atlanta, 1996; and sixteen in Sydney, 2000. In its home Olympics, Australia rose to fourth on the medal tally, behind China, Russia and the United States. And in Athens, in 2004, Australia backed up: seventeen gold and again fourth on the medal table.

Australia had become the new East Germany, the great overperformer. We punched above our weight. However, the culture that produced this success had an unpleasant underside.

At an athletics meet at the AIS, a female athlete performed poorly in a heat. A little later, she began training on an outside track. 'She's a very professional athlete', a coach told ABC Radio, which was covering the event. 'She'll be punishing herself for that performance.' This chilling aside was a small reflection of a wider malaise: a culture of endless striving, the obsessive pursuit of success.

Natalie Cook, who won gold in the beach volleyball in 2000, used Palmolive Gold soap and gold toothpaste, and drove a gold car. She had a gold toaster and a gold-rimmed fish tank, in which goldfish swam among gold trinkets. She sought power from crystals, went firewalking and employed a 'success coach' who rejected any mention of failure: 'That's something average people say'.

In the final of the women's rowing eights in Athens, a member of the Australian team, Sally Robbins, stopped rowing. She later said she had seized up. Other members of the crew accused her of 'mental weakness', and her captain publicly described her as 'this niggle'. In Australia's most successful Olympic Games, the vilification of Sally Robbins was ugly.

Behaviour which in any other field would be seen as a minor personality disorder is actively cultivated in elite sport in order to bring success. As one commentator said of the Robbins' affair: 'We teach people how to win, but not necessarily how to lose'.

The AIS does have policies in place to help its athletes become well-rounded individuals, but the theme of winning is so dominant that it is hard to take these seriously. 'The race for excellence', the institute's website declares, 'has no finish line'. It does have a bottom line, however, and it is a big number.

The Australian Sports Commission is the federal body that oversees sports funding. In 2007–08, $80 million was spent on 'Outcome 1': community participation in sport. 'Outcome 2' is 'excellence in sports performances by Australians', of which the AIS programs are the most important part. It received more than $171 million. In spite of the rhetorical commitment to support sport as part of a healthy lifestyle in the wider community, it is elite sporting programs which consume more than two-thirds of the public money directed to the area.

If there is any self-consciousness among the elite sports about their voracious appetite for funding, it does not show. To the contrary, there is an aggressive culture of entitlement. In 2008 in Beijing, Australia won fourteen gold medals. This meant that we 'fell behind' Great Britain on the medal table. The 'threat' that in 2012, Australia 'may not make its target of a top-five medal tally', brought fresh demands. 'We have to decide up-front whether as a nation we want to be successful', said the chief executive of Rowing Australia. 'If you want to be successful you can't … spread the funding too thinly. We need a quantum leap forward.'

A presumption underlies the rhetoric. We *'have to have'* excellence; the elite sports *'need'* more money. But why?

WHAT PRICE GOLD?

Australian society has been influenced by three main political traditions: conservatism, socialism and liberalism. None lends support to the large-scale use of public funds to nurture elite athletes. To liberals, anyone who wants to compete as an athlete is free to do so, but they will have to find the money themselves. Conservatives agree but honour the values that sport is seen to promote: this might justify a modest subsidy. Socialists are more hostile. Public money is there to meet social needs. One of these needs is community participation in sport, but not expensive elite sports training.

The only justification for programs like those run by the AIS is patriotism, the belief that superiority in sport equates with superiority as a nation.

Before the Montreal Games, one article about Australia's medal prospects was headlined: 'What price gold?' We now know the answer: more than its weight. A study published in 2000 calculated that the twenty-five gold medals won by Australian athletes from the opening of the AIS to 1996 represented about $37 million in public funding *each*. And, unlike in other factories, the unit cost does not decline with greater production: the fourteen gold medals won in Beijing in 2008 cost roughly $48 million each.

Australian sporting success brings pleasure to many people and generates enthusiasm and national pride. But is this really worth such a large amount of money? And is it ultimately more about shoring up a national ego that is more fragile than we want to admit?

+ + +

In 1948, the Olympic Games were held in London. It was a modest event by comparison with most other Olympics—the scars of World War II bombing were still visible, and Britain was still a place of ration cards and shortages. But nonetheless the games were a celebration of the return to normality after the desolation of war.

The Australian team performed modestly, winning three gold medals and finishing fourteenth on the medal table, but it made an excellent impression. 'We have had many very good teams in England over the years, but we've never had a more likeable set of athletes than the "Aussies"', reported the *Times*. 'Their enthusiasm, their willingness to "have a go" at any event and their willingness to advise less finished athletes brought them many friends.'

In the same year, the Australian cricket team, the so-called 'Invincibles' captained by Don Bradman, also toured England. The team went undefeated in twenty-three matches and won the Ashes. A few voices were raised, however, about the team's determination, personified by Bradman, to crush

A few voices were raised, however, about the team's determination, personified by Bradman, to crush every opponent—even weak county sides.

every opponent—even weak county sides. John Arlott, the legendary cricket commentator, dubbed this streak 'Australianism', meaning a 'single-minded determination to win—to win within the laws but, if necessary, to the last limit within them'.

Australia's response to the disappointment of Montreal in 1976 was to forsake the amateur tradition of sportsmanship and take 'Australianism' to new heights. The contrast between the attitude of the 1948 Australian Olympic team and this grim culture of 'excellence' is a sad one.

In terms of human impact, the current drought is the worst in our history. Perhaps it is time to call it the Great Drought. (Fairfax photos)

10
THE GREAT DROUGHT: 2002 TO THE PRESENT

In 1827, the explorer Charles Sturt probed the western plains of New South Wales and encountered a river, which he named after the governor, Ralph Darling. Two years later, Sturt set out to trace the river's course, but there had been a drought and the Darling was now scarcely a river at all; it had ceased to flow.

A century on, Australia's great promoter, Edwin Brady, dismissed Sturt's reports: 'Sturt imagined that he was discovering a drought-stricken desert', but only because he was an ignorant townsman who lacked 'sympathy with Australia'. The Darling, Brady wrote, 'is destined to form the future base for an inland population that will number many more millions than the whole of Australia is carrying at present'.

It was true, said Brady, that there had been some very dry spells, but 'when the rainfall returned, as it inevitably did, to normal, the country recovered its customary fertility with astonishing rapidity'. Irrigation would overcome what occasional water shortages there were, and 'all over Australia men will be masters of the seasons instead of their slaves'.

For a man who boasted of his bush knowledge, Brady had not paid much attention to the weather. The Australian climate is erratic and unpredictable, subject to the 'droughts and flooding rains' Dorothea Mackellar wrote of in 1908.

'The critical need is not to drought-proof the inland', wrote scientist John Williams in 2003, '[but] to help ourselves attain a more realistic and pragmatic appreciation of the character of our continent'. Periodic drought, driven by the El Niño southern oscillation, is part of that character.

Since the 1980s, government policy has tried to encourage farming practice to recognise and adapt to recurrent drought. Financial and other assistance to farmers provided as 'drought relief' is ostensibly predicated on this understanding. The theory is that farmers are expected to manage dry periods, and only in 'exceptional circumstances' will assistance be provided.

Deep down, we still see drought as a deviation from the norm.

The first decade of the twenty-first century has seen this model reduced to absurdity. In mid 2008, a large part of Australia was officially experiencing such exceptional circumstances—some areas had been 'exceptional' for thirteen of the past sixteen years.

Deep down, we still see drought as a deviation from the norm. As one Gippsland farmer told a 2008 inquiry into the social impact of drought, exceptional circumstances funding 'helps to keep unproductive farms unproductive, by rewarding poor management while at the same time, discriminates against and is of no assistance to good operators'.

The strong emotional connection that many farmers have to their properties often causes them to persist in the face of financial reality, and at great cost to themselves and their families. Social scientists call this pattern of stubborn holding-out 'defiant optimism'. A Goulburn farmer was more blunt, calling it the 'ostrich syndrome—people believe that if they put their head down and work harder they'll be able to get themselves out of trouble'.

Disaster is a measure of human impact. Had Cyclone Tracy reached land elsewhere than densely populated Darwin on the northern Australian coastline, it would have been just an extreme weather event. Tracy was a disaster because we built an urban centre that could not survive a cyclone in a place where cyclones happen. By this measure, the current drought—perhaps we can begin to call it the Great Drought—is the worst in our history. We created an agriculture that could not survive severe drought in a place where severe droughts happen.

It is fortunate that the huge inland populations Brady envisaged never eventuated. But still, just under 2 million people live in the Murray-Darling Basin, and perhaps three-quarters depend on agriculture for their livelihoods. Within these communities, the trauma of the current drought has been immense, not least because irrigation was supposed to make their farms 'drought-proof'. Even efficient and previously successful farmers have been forced out of business and off their land. The irrigation community of Colleambally—a rice-growing area created to use the water from the Snowy Mountains Scheme—at one point offered to sell the entire town and its water supply to the federal government.

This disaster was completely predictable. The Darling had already ceased to flow at least once, in 1829. Therefore, it could happen again, especially if large amounts of water were taken from it. If irrigated agriculture extended beyond the capacity of water storages to survive a severe drought, catastrophe would follow. As early as the 1960s, agricultural scientists estimated that irrigation farms covered between double and triple the area that could survive a really bad drought. This reckless expansion, warned one expert, 'may well cause the cost of [future] droughts to be avoidably high'.

In addition, for most of the twentieth century, people who lived in urban areas regarded the water supply as just one more service to be paid for, to be used in whatever way they saw fit. In 1968, CH Munro, a professor of civil engineering at the University of New South Wales, spoke out on Australia's water future. He was scathing of our culture of waste, of how in our large cities 'the use of water for roses and lawns and car washing are taken for granted as essential human needs'.

Munro was provocative for his time—the very idea of water restrictions was seen in the 1960s as politically impossible. But one measure of the magnitude of today's drought is that it has now penetrated the consciousness of those urban Australians Munro spoke of. The fact that water conservation and harvesting have since become common practice, with water being seen more as a precious resource, is welcome. But it reflects poorly on our civic culture, rural and urban alike, that it has taken a catastrophic drought to accept simple realities about the nature of the land on which we live.

Drought and fire are now widely understood as palpable effects of global warming—old disasters with sharper teeth. Crime writer Peter Temple captures the mood of rural

Australia in his novel *The Broken Shore*: 'Fuckin unnatural', says a tough old farmer. 'Startin to believe this greenhouse shit.'

The measurable facts confirm it. Since 1950, there has been an increase in temperature varying from 0.4 degrees Celsius to 0.7 degrees Celsius. There has been more rain in the north-west of the continent and less in the south and east. The sea level has risen by about 70 millimetres.

According to the *Fourth Assessment Report* of the Intergovernmental Panel on Climate Change, the most authoritative scientific body on global warming, the increase in temperature is responsible for the greater severity of droughts in Australia. And it forecasts that worse is to come: heatwaves and bushfires will occur more often and be more severe; floods and droughts are likely to become more frequent and intense; higher temperatures and greater evaporation will increase pressure on water supplies.

The human race is repeating an ancient disaster, resource crash, but this time on a global scale.

Drought, intensified by global warming, is part of a larger story. The human race is repeating an ancient disaster, resource crash, but this time on a global scale.

The most critical threshold being reached is fresh water. There are few untapped sources of water suitable for drinking, agriculture and a host of other industrial uses now essential to human life. More than one billion people lack safe drinking water; more than two billion lack adequate sewerage.

It is possible to desalinate sea water—Australian cities are building plants which will do just that—but the process is expensive and energy-intensive. It is also possible for the use of water in urban areas to become far more efficient. But such measures cannot provide enough water for agriculture.

It is in farming that the most water is used, and the most waste occurs. Large-scale irrigation, from dams or groundwater, initially boosts economic and agricultural output. But the water is often vastly underpriced or given away, and so is wasted. Whole communities come to depend on unsustainable farming practices, making reform politically impossible. Then crisis hits: water tables fall so far that they can no longer be pumped, fields salt up, rivers run dry. What is happening in Australia is happening in India, China, the United States, Canada: the world's food bowls.

+ + +

There is a pattern of ignored warnings that flows through the history of Australian disasters. Time after time, credible people with expert knowledge warned a complacent society that we needed to change our ways. Usually, the response has been a comforting rhetorical formula, bumper-sticker wisdom which ends the discussion:

> The Snowy Mountains Scheme made Australia proud ...
>
> We need protection so that wages and prices are fair ...
>
> Australian soldiers have to stay in France [or Vietnam, or Malaya, or Iraq] until the job is done. And they are doing a great job ...

Australia now faces an environmental crisis, but the reflex responses are still there, the ghosts of old dogma. 'There is plenty of water in Australia, it is just not where we need it.' 'What we need is another Snowy.'

At the time of writing, there is still a political argument taking place about global warming: not over how to best manage the risks it presents, but whether it is happening at all. Many mainstream political leaders question the consensus views of climate scientists, accuse them of bias, and vow to fight anything which will 'cost Australian jobs'. This is the New Protectionism, the belief that we can somehow isolate ourselves, that there can be an Australian economy without a global environment.

Australia now faces an environmental crisis, but the reflex responses are still there, the ghosts of old dogma.

It is possible to draw lessons from history, and if there is one in the Australian experience of disaster, it is that we should listen more to experts.

A stark example stretches in a huge arc across Western Australia, from Geraldton south-east towards Esperance: the Wheatbelt. It was once known as the mallee belt, for the tough scrub which grew there, but in the years after Federation, farmers began to clear the scrub. In the 1920s, an inspecting engineer on the Western Australian railways, WE Wood, was asked to investigate why the boilers in locomotives were rusting more rapidly than expected. Wood found that the water supply drawn from land that had been cleared of native vegetation had become more saline—hence the corrosion. He published a paper arguing that there was a clear connection between land clearing and salinity.

Other Western Australian scientists became conscious of the salt problem. In 1917, a chemist employed by the Department of Agriculture, Thomas Mann, gave evidence to a government inquiry considering new wheat farms. Mann said that because of high salt levels in the soil of many areas proposed for wheat farming, 'agriculture on this land must be considered hazardous'. But the inquiry rejected the expert evidence. It 'strongly' urged that 'scientific prejudice against our mallee lands be not permitted to stand in the way of their being opened up'.

Political opportunism won the day. The mallee was 'opened up': a vast area was cleared of native vegetation between the 1920s and the 1980s. For a time the Wheatbelt was one of Australia's major export-earning regions, but its future is now bleak—it has become one of the worst examples of dryland salinity in the world. Two million hectares are already affected, and another 2 million hectares will soon follow, regardless of remedial measures; the final total area lost to salt desert may well exceed 6 million hectares. Thousands of farmers have been forced off their land, and entire towns are being dragged into economic ruin.

The salinity crisis in the Western Australian Wheatbelt shows in stark relief the pattern of too many Australian disasters. Experts accurately assess a threat and give warning. Popular pressure and ideological blinkers cause politicians to ignore the expert advice. Public opinion favours this decision—until disaster strikes.

To some extent, the problem is political. Australian society leaves politics to a small caste of professionals. Our political parties are machines for winning power, their memberships tiny; branch-level democracy is usually a sober farce. Belonging to a political party is, in general society, seen as a mild eccentricity; for a great many people—journalists, academics, public servants—it is positively frowned on.

The weakness of Australian political parties reflects the weakness of civil society more generally. There are many exceptions, of course: thousands of people give their time, money and energy to schools and kindergartens, to landcare groups and churches, to trade unions and volunteer fire brigades. But many more belong to nothing except a superannuation fund—they are essentially passive consumers of a service called government.

We are also a society which often tries to deal with conflict by avoiding it. A Telstra advertisement for a home broadband connection exemplifies this approach. 'We can all get on when we can all get on' is the campaign's slogan. The poster shows a family which is happy because each member is alone in a separate room, each doing something which involves a plasma screen and an internet connection—family harmony based on having plenty of everything and not needing to talk to each other.

Our national anthem declares that 'for those who come across the sea we've boundless plains to share'. It is easy to share boundless things; much harder is sharing during scarcity, and dealing with the inevitable conflict that arises from it.

At the end of World War II, scientists in the United States conducted an experiment to assess the effects of famine. The Minnesota Semi-starvation Study, as it is often called, placed thirty-six volunteers on a diet intended to reduce their body weight by 25 per cent in three months. Many participants were distressed at how quickly their hunger drove them to selfish, aggressive behaviour. All were conscientious objectors, and most were Christians of strong faith who hoped that the experience would build their spiritual strength. But most reported that semi-starvation 'had coarsened rather than refined them ... they marvelled at how thin their moral and social veneers seemed to be'.

One observer of the experiment wrote: 'Many of the so-called American characteristics—abounding energy, generosity, optimism—became intelligible as the expected behaviour response of a well-fed people'.

Have plentiful food and lots of space allowed us not to solve but to avoid problems?

Is this true of us easygoing, generous Australians too? Have plentiful food and lots of space allowed us not to solve but to avoid problems? In times of plenty, it is possible to live without strong community. We can just spread out in sprawling cities, with fences between our houses, and watch the Olympics on television.

Disasters test the strength of a society, its ability to make hard decisions about allocating resources, to make individual sacrifice for the collective good. Many aspects of Australian life do not prepare us well for the challenges of more frequent and more severe disasters.

We need to change.

SOURCES AND FURTHER READING

INTRODUCTION

For kairos, critical time, see John Carroll, *The Existential Jesus*, Scribe, Melbourne, 2007. For the official view of Australia's past, see *Becoming an Australian Citizen*, Commonwealth of Australia, Canberra, 2007. For the social impacts of disasters, see Allen Barton, *Communities in Disaster: A Sociological Analysis of Collective Stress Situations*, Doubleday, New York, 1969; Christopher Douty, *The Economics of Localised Disaster: The 1906 San Francisco Catastrophe*, Arno Press, San Francisco, 1977; Ted Steinberg, *Acts of God: The Unnatural History of Natural Disaster in America*, Oxford University Press (OUP), Oxford, 2000; and Maria Tumarkin, *Traumascapes: The Power and Fate of Places Transformed by Tragedy*, Melbourne University Publishing (MUP), Melbourne, 2005.

CHAPTER 1

Information on the history of Darwin came from Kathy De La Rue, *The Evolution of Darwin, 1869–1911: A History of the Northern Territory's Capital City during the Years of*

South Australian Administration, Charles Darwin University Press, Darwin, 2004; David Carment, *Looking at Darwin's Past: Material Evidence of European Settlement in Tropical Australia*, North Australia Research Unit, Darwin, 1996; and Ernestine Hill, *The Territory*, Walkabout, Sydney, 1970 (first published 1951). RH Milford's gloomy travelogue was *Australia's Backyards*, Macquarie Head Press, Sydney, 1934. Charles Lowe's report, *Commission of Inquiry into the Circumstances Connected with the Attack Made by Japanese Aircraft on Darwin on 19 February 1942*, Parliament of the Commonwealth of Australia, 1945, is available in digital form through the National Archives of Australia.

A fine oral history of the experience of Cyclone Tracy is Gary McKay, *Tracy: The Storm that Wiped Out Darwin on Christmas Day 1974*, Allen & Unwin, Sydney, 2001. Several of the direct quotations from survivors are taken from this book, which is recommended. Alan Reihar's recollections of Tracy came from his keynote address to the Major Urban Disaster / Civil Defence Study conference, Mt Macedon, Vic. in 1986. For information on the structural damage caused by Tracy, see George Walker, *Report on Cyclone 'Tracy': Effect on Buildings*, 3 vols, James Cook University, Townsville, 1975.

Other recollections of Tracy were taken from George Odgers (ed.), *The Defence Force in the Relief of Darwin after Cyclone Tracy*, Australian Government Publishing Service (AGPS), Canberra, 1980; *Darwin Disaster: Cyclone Tracy: Report by Director-General National Disasters Organisation on the Darwin Relief Operations, 25 December 1974 – 3 January 1975*, AGPS, Canberra, 1975; and Ashleigh Wilson, 'A Perfect

Storm', *Australian*, 18 December 2004. Other sources include Bill Bunbury, *Cyclone Tracy: Picking up the Pieces*, Fremantle Arts Centre Press, Perth, 1994; EA Crane, *Tropical Cyclones*, Heinemann, Melbourne, 1988; *Understanding Cyclones: Northern Territory*, James Cook University, Townsville, 1992; and Alan Stretton, *The Furious Days: The Relief of Darwin*, Sun Books, Melbourne, 1977.

The long-term collective memory of Tracy is discussed in Julie Roberts and Martin Young, 'Transience, Memory and Induced Amnesia: The Re-imagining of Darwin', *Journal of Australian Studies*, vol. 32, no. 1, 2008.

CHAPTER 2

The most important source on the Australian military experience in World War I is the monumental *Official History of Australia in the War of 1914–1918*, 12 vols, Angus & Robertson, Sydney, various dates. The Flanders campaign is described in detail in CEW Bean, *Volume 4, The Australian Imperial Force in France, 1917* (1940). I have also drawn on volumes 3 and 5, both also by Bean, which deal with the AIF in France and Belgium in 1916 and 1918. Bean's work is remarkably accessible for such a detailed history.

The official Anzac Day website is at www.anzacday.org.au. Other quoted material comes from the website of the Western Australian branch of the RSL. For an example of skipping over the worst part of World War I, see *Becoming an Australian Citizen*. For the role of the soldier in national mythology, see Jeff Keshen, 'The Great War Soldier as Nation Builder in Canada and Australia', in Briton B Busch (ed.), *Canada and the Great War*, McGill, Montreal, 2003; and Joan Beaumont, *Australia's War, 1914–1918*, Allen & Unwin, Sydney, 1995.

For the broader political and military context of World War I, see Jeffrey Grey, *A Military History of Australia*, Cambridge University Press (CUP), Cambridge, 1999; Stuart Macintyre, *The Oxford History of Australia, vol. 4, 1901–1942: The Succeeding Age*, OUP, Melbourne, 1986; and Barbara Tuchmann, *The Zimmermann Telegram*, Macmillan, New York, 1966. For a moving account of the disastrous Somme campaign, see Lyn Macdonald, *Somme*, Joseph, London, 1983. The Australian experience is chronicled in Bean, *Volume 3*, and more recent works such as Patrick Lindsay, *Fromelles: Australia's Darkest Day and the Dramatic Discovery of Our Fallen World War One Diggers*, Hardie Grant Books, Melbourne, 2008.

A critical account of the Flanders campaign is Leon Wolff, *In Flanders Fields: The 1917 Campaign*, Longman, London, 1959. I have also drawn from Gary Sheffield and John Bourne (eds), *Douglas Haig: War Diaries and Letters, 1914–1918*, Weidenfeld & Nicolson, London, 2005; Bill Gammage, *The Broken Years: Australian Soldiers in the Great War*, Australian National University Press, Canberra, 1974; and Lyn Macdonald, *They Called it Passchendaele: The Story of the Third Battle of Ypres and of the Men Who Fought in It*, Joseph, London, 1978. The quote which forms the chapter title comes from Gammage.

Other sources include AK MacDougall (ed.), *Letters of General Sir John Monash*, Duffy & Snellgrove, Sydney,

2002; and Geoffrey Searle, *John Monash: A Biography*, MUP, Melbourne, 1990. The quote from Monash about Australian soldiers comes from his book *The Australian Victories in France in 1918*, Lothian, Melbourne, 1920.

For the complex politics of Australia during World War I, see LF Fitzhardinge, *William Morris Hughes: A Political Biography*, Angus & Robertson, Sydney, 1964; Les Carlyon, *The Great War*, Pan Macmillan, Sydney, 2006; Donald Horne, *In Search of Billy Hughes*, Macmillan, Melbourne, 1979; and Peter Spartalis, *The Diplomatic Battles of Billy Hughes*, Hale & Iremonger, Sydney, 1983. Hughes' diatribe on conscription is from 'W.M. Hughes, conscription referendum message' (c. October 1916), ScreenSound Australia, CTN 253356.

World War I produced some haunting poetry. There are many collections and anthologies available. I have quoted from C Day Lewis (ed.), *The Collected Poems of Wilfred Owen*, Chatto & Windus, London, 1963. I also recommend *The Wordsworth Book of First World War Poetry*, Wordsworth, Ware, UK, 1995.

For the postwar climate of censorship, see Peter Coleman, *Obscenity, Blasphemy, Sedition: 100 Years of Censorship in Australia*, Angus & Robertson, Sydney, 1974.

I am indebted to Dr Dan Leach for his interest in this chapter. I have drawn on his unpublished paper 'Destroying Monuments: Counter-memorialisation in European Minority Nationalism' for its discussion of the contested meanings of war memorials, and for information on Flemish separatism. The grief of those bereaved by the war is eloquently expressed in Rudyard Kipling's short story 'The Gardener', first published in 1925 and since much anthologised. An excellent essay on the story's context is Lisa Lewis, 'Notes on "The Gardener"', by Rudyard Kipling', 2004, available online at www.kipling.org.uk.

CHAPTER 3

The composite satellite image of the earth at night was published in *National Geographic* and can be viewed online at http://maps.nationalgeographic.com/maps/print-collection/earth-at-night.html.

For the prehistory of Australia, see Stephen J Pyne, *Burning Bush: A Fire History of Australia*, Henry Holt, New York, 1991; Mary E White, *The Greening of Gondwana*, Reed, Sydney, 1986; and Tim Flannery, *The Future Eaters: An Ecological History of the Australasian Lands and People*, Reed, Melbourne, 1995. For Aboriginal use of fire, see also D Bowman, 'The Impact of Aboriginal Landscape Burning on the Australian Biota', *New Phytologist*, no. 140, 1998.

For the timing of the megafauna extinction, see R Gillespie, 'Updating Martin's Global Extinction Model', *Quaternary Science Reviews*, vol. 27, no. 27-28. Cook's impressions of Australia and Easter Island are from *Captain Cook's Voyages of Discovery*, Everyman's Library, London, 1961. For the story of Easter Island, see Paul Bahn and John Flenley, *Easter Island, Earth Island*, Thames & Hudson, New York, 1992; and Jared Diamond, *Collapse: How Societies Choose to Fail or Succeed*, Viking, New York, 2005, ch. 2. Diamond's book is an excellent study of resource crash across history.

CHAPTER 4

For the history and prehistory of Tasmania, see Henry Reynolds, *Fate of a Free People*, Penguin, Melbourne, 1995; and Clive Turnbull, *Black War: The Extermination of the Tasmanian Aborigines*, Cheshire-Lansdowne, Melbourne, 1965. For life in the penal colony, see *The Hobart Town Gazette and Southern Reporter: A Facsimile Reproduction of Volumes I & II, June 1, 1816 to December 27, 1817*, Trustees of the Public Library of New South Wales, Hobart, 1965; *The Hobart Town Gazette and Southern Reporter: A Facsimile Reproduction of Volumes III & IV, January 3, 1818 to December 25, 1819*, 1967; and James Boyce, *Van Diemen's Land*, Black Inc, Melbourne, 2008. Documents relating to the Emu Bay killing, and to many other aspects of a turbulent period for the colony, can be found in *Historical Records of Australia: Resumed Series III: Despatches and Papers Relating to the History of Tasmania, Vol. IX, Tasmania, January–December 1830*, MUP, Melbourne, 2006. Andrew Bent's article is reprinted in Harry Gordon, *An Eyewitness History of Australia*, 3rd edn, Penguin, Melbourne, 1986. For George Augustus Robinson, see Turnbull; Vivienne Rae-Ellis, *Black Robinson: Protector of Aborigines*, MUP, Melbourne, 1988; and NJB Plomley (ed.), *Friendly Mission: The Tasmanian Journals and Papers of George Augustus Robinson, 1829–1834*, Tasmanian Historical Research Association, Hobart, 1966.

The 1944 special Census which recorded two 'full blood' Aboriginals in Tasmania is cited in JA Alexander (ed.), *Australia 1949: The Herald Year Book*, Herald & Weekly Times, Melbourne, 1949. The United Nations *Convention on the Prevention and Punishment of the Crime of Genocide* is available online at www.hrweb.org/legal/genocide.html. See also S Cohen, 'Human Rights and Crimes of the State: The Culture of Denial', *Australian and New Zealand Journal of Criminology*, vol. 26, 1993.

For conflict between Aborigines and settlers in Victoria, see Richard Broome, *Aboriginal Victorians: A History Since 1800*, Allen & Unwin, Sydney, 2005; and Robert Kenny, *The Lamb Enters the Dreaming: Nathanael Pepper and the Ruptured World*, Scribe, Melbourne, 2007. Kenny's book is fascinating and beautifully written: it's highly recommended. The letter from JG Robertson to CJ La Trobe is reprinted in Manning Clark, *Sources of Australian History*, OUP, London, 1966.

For the argument over the truth or otherwise of the Tasmanian genocide, see Keith Windschuttle, *The Fabrication of Aboriginal History, Vol. 1, Van Diemen's Land 1803–1847*, Macleay Press, Paddington, NSW, 2002; and Robert Manne (ed.), *Whitewash: On Keith Windschuttle's Fabrication of Aboriginal History*, Black Inc, Melbourne, 2003. For an excellent overview of the affair, see Tony Taylor, *Denial: History Betrayed*, MUP, Melbourne, 2008, ch. 6.

CHAPTER 5

Richard Adams' novel *Watership Down* was first published by Penguin in 1973. An animated film appeared in 1978. Both are worth revisiting.

This chapter draws heavily from Eric Rolls' seminal environmental history *They All Ran Wild: The Story of Pests on the Land in Australia*, Angus & Robertson, Sydney, 1969.

Rob Linn, *Battling the Land: 200 Years of Rural Australia*, Allen & Unwin, Sydney, 1999, provides a good overview of the story of Australian agriculture.

For the natural history of rabbits, see Kent Williams, Ian Parer, BJ Coman, John Burley and Mike Brayshaw, *Managing Vertebrate Pests: Rabbits*, CSIRO, Canberra, 1995. Other sources are Catharina Landstram, 'Justifiable Bunnycide: Narrating the Recent Success of Australian Biological Control of Rabbits', *Science as Culture,* vol. 10, no. 2, 2001; Tina Adler, 'Hippity Hop Goes the Virus', *Science News*, vol. 149, no. 13, 1996; and Steve Davidson, 'Australia after Rabbits', *Ecos*, no. 116, 2003.

The story of rabbit-proof fences is told in Rolls; John Pickard, 'Australian Rural Fences: Heritage Challenges for Conserving the Unconservable', *International Journal of Heritage Studies*, vol. 13, no. 6, November 2007; and FK Crowley, *Australia's Western Third: A History of Western Australia from the First Settlements to Modern Times*, Heinemann, Melbourne, 1960.

CHAPTER 6

There is a good-quality reproduction of the painting *Black Thursday* in Madeleine Say, 'Black Thursday: William Strutt's "Itinerent Picture"', *La Trobe Journal*, no. 75, 2005. For a vivid description of Black Thursday, see the beginning of Manning Clark, *A History of Australia, vol. 4, The Earth Abideth for Ever*, MUP, Melbourne, 1978.

The most important accounts of Black Friday are Leonard Stretton, *Report of the Royal Commission to Inquire into the Causes of and Measures Taken to Prevent the Bush Fires of January 1939, and to Protect Life and Property and the Measures to Be Taken to Prevent Bush Fires in Victoria and to Protect Life and Property in the Event of Future Bush Fires*, Victorian Government Printer, Melbourne, 1939; and WS Noble, *Ordeal by Fire: The Week a State Burned Up*, Hawthorn Press, Melbourne, 1977. Other sources are Tom Griffiths, *Secrets of the Forest: Discovering History in Melbourne's Ash Range*, Allen & Unwin, Sydney, 1992; *Forests of Ash: An Environmental History*, CUP, Cambridge, 2001; Paul Collins, *Burn: The Epic Story of Bushfire in Australia*, Allen & Unwin, Sydney, 2006; and Robert Murray and Kate White, *State of Fire: A History of Volunteer Firefighting and the Country Fire Authority in Victoria*, Hargreen, Melbourne, 1995.

For the nature of fire in the Australian environment, see Stephen Pyne, *Burning Bush*; RA Bradstock and JE Williams, *Flammable Australia: The Fire Regimes and Biodiversity of a Continent*, CUP, Cambridge, 2002; Peter Attiwell (ed.), *The Burning Continent: Forest Ecosystems and Fire Management in Australia*, Institute of Public Affairs, Perth, 1994; and Kevin Wareing and David Flinn, *The Victorian Alpine Fires: January–March 2003*, Department of Sustainability and Environment, Melbourne, 2003.

One of the few detailed studies of a major bushfire and its social aftermath in Australia is Roger Lewellyn Wettenhall, *Bushfire Disaster: An Australian Community in Crisis*, Angus & Robertson, Sydney, 1975. See also J Whittaker and D Mercer, 'The Victorian Bushfires of 2002-3 and the Politics of

Blame: A Discourse Analysis', *Australian Geographer*, vol. 35, no. 3, 2004. For the psychological and mental health damage stemming from disaster, see Peter E Hodgkinson and Michael Stewart, *Coping with Catastrophe: A Handbook of Disaster Management*, Routledge, London, 1991.

For the use of dugouts in bushfire, see Peter Evans, 'Forest Fire and Funeral Pyre: Tragedies of the Victorian Bush', *Victorian Naturalist*, vol. 121, no. 3, 2004. Tom Griffiths' essay 'We Have Still Not Lived Long Enough', appeared on the Institute for Social Research website magazine *Inside Story*, 17 June 2009, http://inside.org.au.

CHAPTER 7

The economic causes of the Great Depression are complex and remain the subject of dispute. My interpretation is drawn from the following works: EOG Shann, *An Economic History of Australia*, CUP, Cambridge, 1930; Richard Cotter, 'War, Boom and Depression', in James Griffin (ed.), *Essays in Economic History in Australia*, Jacaranda, Brisbane, 1970; AGL Shaw, *The Economic Development of Australia*, 4th edn, Longmans, Melbourne, 1960; CB Schedvin, *Australia and the Great Depression*, Sydney University Press, Sydney, 1970; and LJ Louis and Ian Turner, *The Depression of the 1930s*, Cassell, Melbourne, 1968. An excellent collection of primary sources on the crash is EOG Shann and DB Copland, *The Crisis in Australian Finance, 1929 to 1931*, Angus & Robertson, Sydney, 1931. A haunting contemporary document is EOG Shann, *The Boom of 1890—and Now: A Call to Australia to*

Put Her House in Order Lest Drought and Falling Prices for Wool and Wheat Overtake Us Again, Cornstalk, Sydney, 1927.

For the social impact of the Depression, see Michael Cannon, *The Human Face of the Great Depression*, Today's Australia, Melbourne, 1997, which is recommended. I have also drawn from Wendy Lowenstein, *Weevils in the Flour: An Oral Record of the 1930s Depression in Australia*, rev. edn, Scribe, Melbourne, 1981; Brian Costar, 'Controlling the Victim: The Authorities and the Unemployed during the Great Depression', *Labour History*, no. 56, October 1989; and Berthia Foott, *Dismissal of a Premier: The Philip Game Papers*, Morgan, Sydney, 1968.

Jack Lang awaits the biographer who can turn his tumultuous life into a really fine book: idea free to a good home. Lang had several tries at a memoir, all marred by factual sloppiness and self-justification: *The Turbulent Years*, Alpha Books, Sydney, 1972, is the best of them. The most authoritative work is Bede Nairn, *The 'Big Fella': Jack Lang and the Australian Labor Party, 1891–1949*, MUP, Melbourne, 1986, but it is a hard slog for the general reader. For the story of the New Guard, see Keith Amos, *The New Guard Movement*, MUP, Melbourne, 1976; and Richard Evans, '"A Menace to This Realm": The New Guard and the New South Wales Police, 1931-32', *History Australia*, vol. 5, no. 3, 2008. The quote from Essington Lewis is from Geoffrey Blainey, *The Steel Master: A Life of Essington Lewis*, rev. edn, Sun Books, Melbourne, 1981.

SOURCES AND FURTHER READING

CHAPTER 8

For typical examples of 'Snowy pride', see 'Snowy Scheme to Be a National Treasure', *Advertiser* (Adelaide), 8 July 2001; Brad Collis, 'Heavy Symbolism Almost Outweighs Size of the Scheme', *Age*, 3 August 2006; Danielle Woolage, 'Frankly, This Is Australia's Finest Work', *Illawarra Mercury*, 8 August 2001; and Charles Meeking, *Snowy Mountains Conquest: Harnessing the Waters of Australia's Highest Mountains*, Hutchinson, Melbourne, 1968. For an insightful study of the construction of the Snowy myth, see Grahame Griffin, 'Selling the Snowy: The Snowy Mountains Scheme and National Mythmaking', *Journal of Australian Studies*, no. 79, 2003.

Edwin Brady's *Australia Unlimited*, George Robertson, Melbourne, 1918, is huge, running to more than 1000 pages. A beautiful book, it is far better illustrated than it is written. CJ Dennis' *The Songs of a Sentimental Bloke*, Angus & Robertson, Sydney, 1960, was first published in 1915. The school textbook mentioned is CS Browne, *Australia: A General Account*, Thomas Nelson and Sons, London, 1929.

For the psychology of closer settlement, see Marc Brodie, 'The Politics of Rural Nostalgia between the Wars', in Graeme Davison and Marc Brodie (eds), *Struggle Country: The Rural Ideal in Twentieth Century Australia*, Monash University ePress, Melbourne, 2005.

The information about William Hudson is from Alistair Mant, *Intelligent Leadership*, Allen & Unwin, Sydney, 1999; and Eric Sparke, 'Sir William Hudson', *Australian Dictionary of Biography*, MUP, Melbourne, 1996.

HC Coombs' speech on postwar reconstruction was published in DAS Campbell (ed.), *Post-War Reconstruction in Australia*, Australasian Publishing, Sydney, 1944. For background to the Dneiper dam, see Peter Kenez, *A History of the Soviet Union from the Beginning to the End*, CUP, Cambridge, 1999.

For the politics of starting the Snowy, see Mant, *Intelligent Leadership*; Lionel Wigmore, *Struggle for the Snowy: The Background of the Snowy Mountains Scheme*, OUP, London, 1968; and David Day, *Chifley*, HarperCollins, Sydney, 2002. The taxation revenue of Australia's governments for 1947 is recorded in *Australia 1949: The Herald Year Book*.

More critical perspectives on the Snowy emerged from the early 1960s. See 'Murrumbidgee Irrigation: A Regional Study', *Current Affairs Bulletin*, vol. 31, no. 10, 1963; 'The Snowy – An Appraisal', *Current Affairs Bulletin*, vol. 31, no. 13, 1963; 'Snowy Power and Murrumbidgee Irrigation: Two Replies', *Current Affairs Bulletin*, vol. 32, no. 7, 1963; and BR Davidson, *Australia Wet or Dry?: The Physical and Economic Limits of the Expansion of Irrigation*, MUP, Melbourne, 1969. A detailed assessment from the 1980s is John J Pigram, *Issues in the Management of Australia's Water Resources*, Longman Cheshire, Sydney, 1986.

For the ecological damage caused by the scheme, see Tim Flannery, 'Beautiful Lies', *Quarterly Essay*, no. 9, 2003; and John J Pigram, 'Options for Rehabilitation of Australia's Snowy River: An Economic Perspective', *Regulated Rivers: Research & Management*, vol. 16, no. 4, 2000.

SOURCES AND FURTHER READING

CHAPTER 9

The best overview of the development of Australian elite sports is Brett Hutchins, 'The Opening of the Australian Institute of Sport: The Government Takes Control of the National Pastime', in Martin Crotty and David Andrew Roberts (eds), *Turning Points in Australian History*, University of New South Wales Press, Sydney, 2009. The Australian Institute of Sport website has a brief official history by Matthew Eggins, modestly titled 'History and Successes: The AIS—An Icon for Excellence in Sport', www.ausport.gov.au/ais/history.

The media coverage of the Montreal Olympics comes primarily from the Melbourne *Age* over July 1976.

For discussions of the place of elite sport as opposed to community sport, see Gordon Waitt, 'The Olympic Spirit and Civic Boosterism: The Sydney 2000 Olympics', *Tourism Geographies*, vol. 3, no. 3, 2001; Mick Green, 'Olympic Glory or Grassroots Development?: Sport Policy Priorities in Australia, Canada and the United Kingdom, 1960-2006', *International Journal of the History of Sport*, vol. 24, no. 7, 2007; and S Brookes and J Wiggan, 'Reflecting the Public Value of Sport', *Public Management Review*, vol. 11, no. 4, 2009.

Information on the cost of elite sports programs comes from the Australian Sports Commission, *Annual Report 2007-08*, and from Hutchins. Medal tallies can be viewed at the International Olympic Committee website, www.olympic.org. An odd but interesting perspective on medal counts is AB Bernard and MR Busse, 'Who Wins the Olympic Games:

Economic Resources and Medal Totals', *Review of Economics and Statistics*, vol. 86, no. 1, 2004.

For details on the East German athletics program, see 'German Athletics Coaches Admit East German Doping Past', *Deutsche Welle*, 7 April 2009; and Jonathan Grix, 'The Decline of Mass Sport Provision in the German Democratic Republic', *International Journal of the History of Sport*, vol. 25, no. 4, 2008.

I heard the ABC *Grandstand* broadcast in which a coach talked of an athlete 'punishing herself': I am quoting from memory. For Natalie Cook's intense approach to competing, see Michelle Griffin, 'There Comes a Time When Too Much Sports Psychology Is Barely Enough', in Garrie Hutchinson (ed.), *The Best Australian Sports Writing 2004*, Black Inc., Melbourne, 2004. A no-less-chilling discussion of 'excellence' is Paul R Appleton, Howard K Hall, and Andrew P Hill, 'Relations between Multidimensional Perfectionism and Burnout in Junior-elite Male Athletes', *Psychology of Sport & Exercise*, vol. 10, no. 4, 2009.

The quote from Pierre de Coubertin and the item from *The Times* of London about the Australian 1948 Olympic team both come from *Australia 1949: The Herald Year Book*.

CHAPTER 10

For Sturt's explorations, see 'Drought', *Current Affairs Bulletin*, vol. 38, no. 4, 1966; and Manning Clark, *A History of Australia, vol. 2: New South Wales and Van Diemen's Land*, MUP, Melbourne, 1968. Edwin Brady's work is cited above.

For an understanding of the complexities of the Australian climate, I have looked to Patrick Troy (ed.), *Troubled Waters: Confronting the Water Crisis in Australia's Cities*, ANU E Press, Canberra, 2008; B O'Meagher, M Stafford Smith and DH White, 'Approaches to Integrated Drought Risk Management', in DA Wilhite (ed.), *Drought*, Routledge, Montreal, 2000; RL Heathcote, '"She'll Be Right, Mate": Coping with Drought, Strategies Old and New in Australia', in ibid; Peter Kenny and Drought Policy Review Expert Social Panel Australia, *It's About People: Changing Perspectives on Dryness: A Report to Government*, Department of Agriculture, Fisheries and Forestry, Canberra, 2008.

For the limitations of irrigation in mitigating drought, see BR Davidson, *Australia Wet or Dry?*. On the urban water crisis, see CH Munro, *The Future Conservation of Australia's Water Resources*, University of Sydney, Sydney, 1969.

For the threat of global resource crash, see Elino Ostrom, 'Revisiting the Commons: Local Lessons, Global Challenges', *Science*, no. 284, 1999; Mike Davis, *Planet of Slums*, Verso, London, 2006; and Fen Montaigne, 'Water Pressure', *National Geographic*, September 2002. For the problem of food production, see Joel Bourne, 'The End of Plenty', *National Geographic*, June 2009.

The Western Australian salinity disaster is described in detail in Quentin Beresford, Hugo Bekle, Harry Phillips and Jane Murlock, *The Salinity Crisis: Landscapes, Communities and Politics*, University of Western Australia Press, Perth, 2001.

The best accessible account of the science of global warming is Tim Flannery, *We Are the Weather Makers: The Story of Global Warming*, Text, Melbourne, 2006. For a detailed overview of the science, see *The Fourth Assessment Report of the Intergovernmental Panel on Climate Change*, CUP, Cambridge, 2007; chapter 11 focuses on Australia and New Zealand. The quote from Peter Temple is in *The Broken Shore*, Text, Melbourne, 2005.

ACKNOWLEDGEMENTS

This book would not have been possible without the assistance and support of many people. I am particularly grateful to my employer, the Institute for Social Research at Swinburne University of Technology, Melbourne, for allowing me time for research and writing. I am especially grateful to Professor Denise Meredyth for her support.

My publisher Elisa Berg at Melbourne University Publishing has been an extraordinary help: supportive, rigorous, helpful and critical, all in the right measure. I am grateful for her continual input, and to Paul Smitz and Kabita Dhara for their skilled editing.

Friends, family and colleagues too numerous to name have shown interest in the project, and contributed ideas or suggested sources: you know who you are, thank you all. I especially want to thank my father, Ray Evans, who will disagree strongly with parts of this book, but whose love, generosity and unflagging interest in my work is deeply appreciated.

Writing this book in a short space of time has placed a great burden on others. I could not have finished it without the continual love, support, patience and understanding of my wife Heather and my daughters Rose and Zoë. My heartfelt love and thanks: you are my joy.

I give thanks to God for the amazing world in which we live, for my family, and for the opportunity to write about such rich human stories.